This Is Not Sufficient

LEONARD LAWLOR

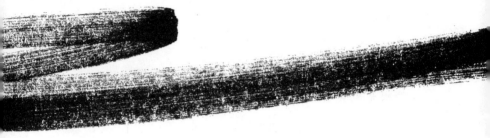

This Is Not Sufficient

An Essay on **Animality and**
Human Nature in Derrida

COLUMBIA UNIVERSITY PRESS   NEW YORK

Columbia University Press
Publishers Since 1893
New York   Chichester, West Sussex

Copyright © 2007 Columbia University Press

Library of Congress Cataloging-in-Publication Data
Lawlor, Leonard, 1954–
    This is not sufficient : an essay on animality and human nature in Derrida /
Leonard Lawlor.
        p. cm.
    Includes bibliographical references and index.
    ISBN 978-0-231-14312-7
    1. Derrida, Jacques. 2.   Animals (Philosophy) 3. Psychology.   4. Human
behavior.   I. Title.

    B2430.D484L39   2007
    194—dc22

Columbia University Press books are printed on permanent and
durable acid-free paper.
Printed in the United States of America

c 10 9 8 7 6 5 4 3 2 1

FOR JONATHAN

CONTENTS

ABBREVIATIONS

Reference is always made first to the original French, then to the
English translation. At times, I have modified published English
translations, and, unless otherwise noted, translations from the
French are my own.

A   *L'animal que donc je suis*. Paris: Galilée, 2006.

AAEL   *Adieu à Emmanuel Levinas*. Paris: Galilée, 1997. English trans-
       lation by Michael Naas and Pascale-Anne Brault, as *Adieu to
       Emmanuel Levinas*. Stanford, Calif.: Stanford University Press,
       1999.

AP   *Apories*. Paris: Galilée, 1996. English translation by Thomas
       Dutoit, as Aporias. Stanford, Calif.: Stanford University Press,
       1993.

ASAR   "And Say the Animal Responded" [chap. 3 of *L'animal que donc
       je suis*], trans. David Wills, in Zoontologies: The Question of
       the Animal, ed. Cary Wolfe, 121–146. Minneapolis: University
       of Minnesota Press, 2003.

ATIA   "The Animal that Therefore I Am (More to Follow)" [chap. 1 of
       L'animal que donc je suis], trans. David Wills, Critical Inquiry
       28 (Winter 2002): 369–418.

B   *Béliers*. Paris: Galilée, 2003. English translation by Thomas Du-
        toit and Philippe Romanski, as "Rams," in *Sovereignties in Ques-
        tion: The Poetics of Paul Celan*, ed. Thomas Dutoit and Outi Pas-
        anen, 135–163. New York: Fordham University Press, 2005.

CF   *Chaque fois unique, la fin du monde*. Paris: Galilée, 2003. Origi-
        nally published in English as *The Work of Mourning*. Ed.
        Pascale-Anne Brault and Michael Naas. Chicago: University of
        Chicago Press, 2001.

CNPP   "Comment ne pas parler: Dénégations (1986)." In *Psyché: In-
        ventions de l'autre*, 535–595. Paris: Galilée, 1987. English transla-
        tion by Ken Frieden, as "How to Avoid Speaking: Denials," in
        Languages of the Unsayable, ed. Sanford Budick and Wolfgang
        Iser, 3–70. New York: Columbia University Press, 1989.

CS11   *Le "concept" du 11 septembre: Dialogues à New York (octobre–
        décembre 2001) avec Giovanna Borradori*. With Jürgen Haber-
        mas. Paris: Galilée, 2004. Originally published in English as
        *Philosophy in the Time of Terror: Dialogues with Jürgen Haber-
        mas and Jacques Derrida*. Chicago: University of Chicago Press,
        2003.

D   *Demeure*. Paris: Galilée, 1998. English translation by Elizabeth
        Rottenberg, as "Demeure: Fiction and Testimony," in Maurice
        Blanchot, *The Instant of My Death*, 13–102. Stanford, Calif.:
        Stanford University Press, 2000.

DIS   *La dissemination*. Paris: Seuil, 1972. English translation by Bar-
        bara Johnson, as *Dissemination*. Chicago: University of Chi-
        cago Press, 1981.

DLE   *De l'esprit*. Paris: Galilée, 1987. English translation by Geoff
        Bennington and Rachel Bowlby, as *Of Spirit*. Chicago: Univer-
        sity of Chicago Press, 1989.

DLG   *De la grammatologie*. Paris: Minuit, 1967. English translation
        by Gayatri Spivak, as *Of Grammatology*. Baltimore: Johns Hop-
        kins University Press, 1974.

DM   "Donner la mort." In *L'éthique du don: Jacques Derrida et la
        pensée du don*, 11–108. Paris: Transition, 1992. English transla-
        tion by David Wills, as *The Gift of Death*. Chicago: University
        of Chicago Press, 1995.

DQD *De quoi demain . . . Dialogue.* Paris: Fayard/Galilée, 2001. English translation by Jeff Fort, as *For What Tomorrow . . . A Dialogue.* Stanford, Calif.: Stanford University Press, 2004.

ECM "At This Very moment in This Work Here I Am." In *Re-Reading Levinas,* ed. Robert Bernasconi and Simon Critchley, 11–47. Bloomington: Indiana University Press, 1991. Original French can be found in *Psyché: Inventions de l'autre,* 159–202.

ED *L'écriture et la différence.* Paris: Seuil, 1967. English translation by Alan Bass, as *Writing and Difference.* Chicago: University of Chicago Press, 1978.

FL *Force de loi.* Paris: Galilée, 1994; English translation by Mary Quaintance, as "Force of Law: The Mystical Foundation of Authority," in *Deconstruction and the Possibility of Justice,* ed. Drucilla Cornell, Michael Rosenfeld, and David Gray Carlson, 3–67. New York: Routledge, 1992.

FS "Foi et savoir." In *La Religion,* ed. Jacques Derrida and Gianni Vattimo, 9–86. Paris: Seuil, 1996. English translation by Samuel Weber, as "Faith and Knowledge," in *Religion,* ed. Jacques Derrida and Gianni Vattimo, 1–78. Stanford, Calif.: Stanford University Press, 1998.

GL *Glas.* 2 vols. Paris: Denoël/Gontheier, 1981 [1974]. English translation by John P. Leavey, Jr., and Richard Rand, as *Glas.* Lincoln: University of Nebraska Press, 1986.

GS2 "La main de Heidegger (*Geschlecht* II) (1984–1985)." In *Psyché,* 415–452. Paris: Galilée, 1987. English translation by John P. Leavey, Jr., as "*Geschlecht* II: Heidegger's Hand," in *Deconstruction and Philosophy,* ed. John Sallis, 161–196. Chicago: University of Chicago Press, 1987.

GS4 "L'oreille de Heidegger: Philopolémologie (*Geschlecht* IV)." In *Politiques de l'amitié,* 343–419. Paris: Galilée, 1994. English translation by John P. Leavey, Jr., as "Heidegger's Ear: Philopolemology (Geschlecht IV)," in *Reading Heidegger: Commemorations,* 163–218. Bloomington: Indiana University Press, 1993.

K *Khôra.* Paris: Galilée, 1993. English translation by Ian McLeod, as "Khôra," in *On the Name,* ed. Thomas Dutoit, 89–127. Stanford, Calif.: Stanford University Press, 1995: 89–127.

LI   *Limited Inc.* Paris: Galilée, 1990. Originally published in English as *Limited Inc.*, trans. Samuel Weber. Evanston, Ill.: Northwestern University Press, 1988 [1977].

MDA   *Mémoires d'aveugle: L'autoportrait et autres ruines.* Paris: Editions de la Réunion des musées nationaux, 1990. English translation by Pascale-Anne Brault and Michael Naas, as *Memories of the Blind: The Self-Portrait and Other Ruins.* Chicago: University of Chicago Press, 1993.

MDM   *Mémoires pour Paul de Man.* Paris: Galilée, 1988. Originally published in English as *Memoires for Paul de Man.* Trans. Cecile Lindsay, Jonathan Culler, and Eduardo Cadava. New York: Columbia University Press, 1986.

MLA   *Le monolinguisme de l'autre.* Paris: Galilée, 1996. English translation by Patrick Mensah, as *Monolingualism of the Other.* Stanford, Calif.: Stanford University Press, 1998.

MP   *Marges de la philosophie.* Paris: Minuit, 1972. English translation by Alan Bass, as *Margins of Philosophy.* Chicago: University of Chicago Press, 1982.

ORH   "On Reading Heidegger: An Outline of Remarks to the Essex Colloquium." *Research in Phenomenology* 27 (1987): 171–185.

PA   *Politiques de l'amitié.* Paris: Galilée, 1994. English translation by George Collins, as *Politics of Friendship.* London: Verso, 1997.

PC   *La carte postale de Socrate à Freud et au-delà.* Paris: Flammarion, 1980. English translation by Alan Bass, as *The Postcard from Socrates to Freud and Beyond.* Chicago: University of Chicago Press, 1987.

POS   *Positions.* Paris: Minuit, 1972. English translation by Alan Bass, as *Positions.* Chicago: University of Chicago Press, 1981.

PS   *Points de suspension: Entretiens.* Paris: Galilée, 1992. English translation by Peggy Kamuf and others, as *Points . . . Interviews, 1974–1994,* ed. Elizabeth Weber. Stanford, Calif.: Stanford University Press, 1995.

RME   "Le ruban de machine à ecrire." In *Papier Machine,* 33–104. Paris: Galilée, 2001. English translation by Peggy Kamuf, as "Typewriter Ribbon," in *Without Alibi,* 71–160.

RPS *Résistances de la psychanalyse.* Paris: Galilée, 1996. English translation by Peggy Kamuf, Pascale-Anne Brault, and Michael Naas, as *Resistances of Psychoanalysis.* Stanford, Calif.: Stanford University Press, 1998.

SM *Spectres de Marx.* Paris: Galilée, 1993. English translation by Peggy Kamuf, as *Specters of Marx.* New York: Routledge, 1994.

SN *Sauf le nom.* Paris: Galilée, 1993. English translation in *On the Name*, ed. Thomas Dutoit, 89–127. Stanford, Calif.: Stanford University Press, 1995.

SPC *Schibboleth pour Paul Celan.* Paris: Galilée, 1986. English translation by Joshua Wilner, revised by Thomas Dutoit, as "Schibboleth: For Paul Celan," in *Sovereignties in Question: The Poetics of Paul Celan*, ed. Thomas Dutoit and Outi Pasanen, 1–64. New York: Fordham University Press, 2005.

TJLN *Le toucher: Jean-Luc Nancy.* Paris: Galilée, 2000. English translation by Christine Irizarry, as *On Touching—Jean-Luc Nancy.* Stanford, Calif.: Stanford University Press, 2005.

V *Voyous.* Paris: Galilée, 2003. English translation by Pascale-Anne Brault and Michael Naas, as *Rogues.* Stanford, Calif.: Stanford University Press, 2005.

VP *La voix et le phénomène.* Paris: Presses Universitaires de France, 1983 [1967]. English translation by David B. Allison, as *Speech and Phenomena.* Evanston, Ill.: Northwestern University Press, 1973.

ACKNOWLEDGMENTS

The book is based on three lectures given at the Collegium Phaenomenologicum, Città di Castello, Umbria, Italy, on July 24, 26, and 28, 2006. I cannot thank Michael Naas enough for having invited me to present these lectures and for his friendship; he also read an earlier draft of the manuscript and made many helpful comments.

I would like to thank all the participants and faculty who were present at the 2006 Collegium, in particular, Joshua Andresen, Geoff Bennington, Peg Birmingham, Louise Burchill, Marcus Coelen, Olivia Custer, Françoise Dastur, Marc Djabbalah, Maxime Doyon, Jonathan Dronsfield, Chris Eagle, Edo Evink, Russell Ford, Kathryn Gines, Lisa Guenther, Martin Hägglund, Samir Haddad, Dana Hollander, Larry Hatab, Ryan Hellmers, Samuel Ijsseling, Mike Jonik, Peggy Kamuf, Sina Kramer, Don Landes, Rick Lee, Ken Lieberman, Paul Livingston, Bill Martin, Scott Marratto, Holly Moore, Barbara Muraca, Pat O'Connor, Jeff Pardikes, Francois Raffoul, Elizabeth Rottenberg, John Sallis, Alan Schrift, Brian Schroeder, Robert Vallier, Ben Vedder, Cory Wimberley, and David Wood.

I would also like to thank all the students in my Derrida seminar at the University of Memphis during the spring semester of 2006; certain of these students also attended the Collegium: Bryan Bannon, Cheri Carr, Erinn Gilson, and John Nale. Brien Karas, who participated in the seminar, made penetrating comments during the entire writing process, from the composition of the lectures to the revisions for the final submission of this manuscript.

Fred Evans and Zeynep Direk read an early draft of chapters 1 and 3 and offered very helpful comments. In the philosophy department at Memphis, Sarah Clark Miller provided a different viewpoint on the question of animal suffering. Ted Toadvine also made helpful comments, as did Antonio Calcagno and Diane Ens. My thanks to Fred, Zeynep, Sarah, Ted, Antonio, and Diane.

Rodolphe Gasché read an earlier draft of the manuscript and made helpful comments; I cannot thank him enough for all the support he has given me over many years.

I have presented versions of the lectures in Istanbul, Winnipeg, and Stockholm. My thanks to Elif Yavnik in Istanbul; to Dawne Macance and Lisa Muirhead at the University of Manitoba in Winnipeg; and to Eric Alliez, Cathy Caruth, Leif Dahlberg, Jari Kauppinen, Jakob Nilsson, Cecilia Parsberg, Hans Ruin, Cecilia Sjöholm, Fredrika Spindler, Björn Thorsteinsson, and Sven-Olaf Wallenstein in Stockholm.

I am grateful to Wendy Lochner, who provided essential help at Columbia University Press.

As always, I must thank everyone in the philosophy department at the University of Memphis. In particular, Cathy Wilhelm was an immense help.

Finally, I must thank my family, Jennifer, Jonathan, and Casey, for their patience and support while I was writing this text.

This Is Not Sufficient

Introduction

The Order: Be Incorruptible

The text that you are about to read attempts to think with Derrida; indeed, it attempts to follow him.[1] We are going to follow Derrida not as an animal to be captured but as a friend who lays out a path for us, a friend who gives us an imperative, a friend who gives us an order. This order will unfold in three ways. First, we shall think along with Derrida in regard to one specific problem: the problem of the suffering of animals in today's world. That animals suffer today is undeniable, which means that one can only deny that suffering and deny it, that is, respond to it, in countless ways. What we are seeking, as you shall see in a moment, is a more sufficient response to the undeniable suffering of animals. More sufficient than what?

There are two extreme responses, both completely insufficient. On the one hand, there is the response that gives to animals the same properties that humans possess; doing so requires that we show identical compassion to animals as to humans since animals and humans form a continuous species. The other response, equally insufficient, consists in reducing animals to machines; doing so requires no compassion from us since in this view animals are a species that is separate from us.[2] Here I think it is necessary to say that what Derrida did in the book *L'animal que donc je suis*[3] is in alliance with what Peter Singer did in his 1975 *Animal Liberation*.[4] Like Singer, Derrida invokes Bentham's question regarding animals: do they suffer (A 48/ATIA 396).[5] Like Derrida, Singer does not use the idea of rights to ground his attack on what he calls "speciesism" (a word he coins based on the words "racism" and "sexism").[6] If you accept this alliance, therefore, and you want to follow Derrida, then you must, we must, support and advocate what Peter Singer (among others) supports and advocates.[7] We must alleviate animal suffering by changing their conditions on farms, by changing their conditions in laboratories. We must make these direct attacks. I think that we must practice asceticism, some form of vegetarianism, a vegetarianism that, as I shall show, turns out to be a form of "carnivorism."[8] You have to eat, after all, but let us try to eat in the least violent way. This transformed sense of eating means internalizing animals, letting them in, and, especially, not sacrificing them for our sakes. Although I will advocate a kind of recipe for eating well, I will not advocate specific and concrete reforms. Such reforms must be made on the local level, it seems to me, where cultural differences can be taken into account. No matter what, however, these reforms, any reforms, are not sufficient in order to respond to animal suffering. No reform will ever be sufficient. What I am advocating is more modest than a new set of laws or values aiming to determine human behavior in relation to animals. I am hoping—and this is perhaps all a philosopher can hope for in his or her writings—to change people's perceptions and attitudes toward our relation to animals. All a philosopher or, more generally, a thinker (a poet perhaps) can provide is, as Deleuze and Guattari would say, "the constellation of an event to come."[9] I hope that what follows will provide a framework, the recipe, in which we can think about our relation to animals in a new way. This framework, since I am following Derrida, amounts to affirming unconditional hospitality.

Second, what we are going to do here is think along with Derrida by going down the path of anti-Platonism. I think we have to recognize that, since the time of Nietzsche, the project of anti-Platonism has dominated our philosophical work. A very clear sign that the project of anti-Platonism still dominates our today is the widespread and virtually unquestioned acceptance of naturalism in analytic philosophy. Another clear sign is the current struggle between secularism and religious fundamentalism (whether it be Christian, Islamic, or even Hindu) (see V 51–52/28). Finally, there is one more sign. Satellites manufactured by humans encircle the earth, connecting every surface to every other.[10] In other words, by means of globalization, we are no longer in the world but rather the world is enclosed in the globe of human existence. This phrase "in the world," of course, alludes to Heidegger. Heidegger prescribed that we must "twist free" of Platonism, which means that not only Platonism must be overcome but also anti-Platonism since it is the mere reversal of Platonism. It seems to me that, in order to twist free of Platonism, we cannot be naturalists. Instead, we must be, as Derrida says in *Rogues*, "responsible guardians of the heritage of transcendental idealism" (V 188/134).[11] It is only through transcendental idealism that we can reach what Deleuze calls immanence. The formula for immanence that I am following comes from Deleuze and Guattari's *What Is Philosophy?* Immanence is a plane that precedes or is prior to the separation between subject and object, prior to the separation between matter and memory (or consciousness).[12] By stressing immanence, perhaps we are not really following Derrida, but following is never blind obedience to a program. Derrida, in contrast to Deleuze, speaks of transcendence. Yet, if we must speak of transcendence, this transcendence will always be a transcendence within immanence, a transcendence that is right on immanence (or we could use the French adverb "à même," rendered as "right on," which combines the "à" or "to" of transcendence and the "même" or "same" of immanence).[13] This point concerning transcendence is especially important if we want to understand Derrida's relation to Christianity, a relation that we could call, borrowing from Nancy, a "deconstruction of Christianity."[14]

But even with laying some transcendence right on immanence, we must recognize that immanence refers to an experience, the experience of autoaffection. It is well known that Heidegger had interpreted the transcendental schematism in Kant as autoaffection.[15] This interpretation sets up all the discussions of autoaffection in the twentieth century and now into the twenty-first century. Yet autoaffection has always defined life. Immanence, then, is equivalent to life, to a life or to one life, as Deleuze would say. As we shall see, the indefinite and yet singular article in the phrase "a life" will be important. We must confront an important conceptual question immediately. What is a singularity? A singularity is not a particular that we are able to classify under a general concept. No mental representation can be formed of it, although a singularity is not alien to a representation. A singularity cannot be translated, although translation is not alien to it. A singularity is informal, although formalization is not alien to it. A singularity is not external to repeatability; it is the outside of repeatability. A singularity is a "boiling point," as Deleuze would say, or it is a "statement," as Foucault would say. Here is a statement: "I am afraid to die." Every time anyone utters or gestures toward the fear of death, we have a statement. A singularity is an event, a "once and for all." It is a discontinuity. A singularity is irreplaceable, and there can be no substitute for it, as Derrida would say. It is a date, the day on which the crocuses come up in the spring, the eighth of April. It is the day on which one's parents die, not both, just one, but the one being dead kills the other. This world goes away and with it the individuation that comes from one's proper name. Only under this condition of losing one's individuation, however, is it possible for one to assume one's proper name. This taking-up of one's proper name crosses through with an X the singularity of the event—and this crossing-through must happen—but the tracing-through of the event refers back to the event and refers ahead to the event to come. Through loss, the tracing works. Understood through this loss or privation of singularity, life therefore must be conceived in terms of powerlessness. There is a kind of mortalism within life. (I am taking this word "mortalism" from Foucault's *The Birth of the Clinic*.)[16] There is a kind of weakness in the heart of power, a blindness in the middle of the power of vision, a disappearance within appearance, a fault that cracks along the line of singularity and iterability (universalization: the repetition of the statement or the name), a fault that makes it necessary for us to act.[17] There is finally, I think, no greater problem for thought today than the problem of how to conceive life in terms of powerlessness. We can see a larger issue developing here. The question of how to conceive life forces us to conceive the living, all living beings, including us.

Finally, in this text I am attempting to continue and protect the ethos that produced the thought that I am here following, the thought of Derrida, of course, but also, as you can see, the thought of Deleuze and Foucault. We must continue and protect the ethos that produced Derrida, Deleuze, and Foucault, especially now that we are left only with their works. These thinkers could not be corrupted by the pressure of the academy to conform to the normal modes of thinking; they could not be corrupted by the ridicule of public opinion. If we are to follow them, we must engage is an ethos of fearless questioning. We must engage in an ethos that is an ethos of paradox and aporia. We must "contest," as Foucault would say, the dogmatism of metaphysics as well as the dogmatism of common sense. We must "deconstruct," as Derrida, of course, would say, and we must "construct," as Deleuze would say, new concepts, new peoples, new forms of life. We who follow these great thinkers, we must be like them; we, or better, *you* must be a new generation of "incorruptibles."

A More Sufficient Response

Is it possible to define Derrida's thought with a simple sentence? Perhaps one could say this: Derrida is and always has been a thinker of today. Already in 1968, before the end of the cold war, Derrida had called our attention to what was happening on that today. At the beginning of "The Ends of Man," Derrida comments on the increasing number of international philosophy colloquia starting in the second half of the twentieth century; he diagnoses this phenomenon as an attempt by the West to master those places where the discussion of philosophical issues makes no sense (MP 133/112–113). It is as if Derrida had already started to think about globalization—a word that did not exist in 1968— through the idea of the international philosophy conference. Yet there is more. In these opening pages of "The Ends of Man," Derrida also speaks of democracy as the only form in which such colloquia can take place because only democracy can contain a diversity of languages and nations. And yet Derrida argues that the form of democracy, a form in which he is granted permission to protest against the Vietnam War, is not adequate to the idea of democracy (MP 134–135/114). It is as if in 1968 Derrida had already found the thought of "democracy to come." Nearly forty years later, in *Rogues*, Derrida will link, as in "The Ends of Man," the thought of democracy to come with "the age of so-called *mondialisation*," with "globalization," as is said in anglophone world (V 11–12/xii–xiii). Late in the second essay of *Rogues*, "The 'World' of the Enlightenment to Come," Derrida tells us that "mondialisation" makes war, especially world war, lose its pertinence (V 212/154). War losing its pertinence, however, does not imply peace (V 174/124). Derrida says, "A new violence is being prepared and in truth has been unleashed for some time now, in a way that is more visibly suicidal . . . than ever" (V 214/156). His reflections on suicide (or the autoimmune, as he adds here), refer us to the question of life.[18] In *Rogues* again, he says, "the old word 'vie' [life] perhaps remains the enigma of the political around which we turn" (V 22/4). It is necessary, therefore, to think "life otherwise, life and the force of life" (V 57/33). To do this, we must think about the living, *le vivant*, in French, *anima* in Latin, and that leads us to animals. In his dialogue with Elizabeth Roudinesco, Derrida is emphatic about the decisive nature of the question of animality; he says, "[the question of animality] represents the limit upon which all the great questions are formed and determined, as well as the concepts that attempt to delimit what is 'proper to man,' the essence and the future of humanity, ethics, politics, law, 'human rights,' 'crimes against humanity,' 'genocide,' etc." (DQD 106/63).[19] Even if globalization has led to the universal expansion of human rights, it is still rational "to continue to interrogate . . . all the limits we thought pertained to life . . . between the living and the dead . . . , but also between that living being called 'human' and the one called 'animal'" (V 209/151; see also FL 62–63/28–29).

Here I will attempt precisely that: to think about, with Derrida, the limit between the living being called man and the one called animal. This is a thought, once more, of "the ends of man," once more a question of who we are. This thinking will lead, I hope, to a different concept of "life and the force of life." Force will always be at the center of the question of life. If, on the basis of Aristotle, life has been thought as pure actuality or presence, as the full and proper possession of all one's powers and possibilities, as the prime mover, autoaffection in the form of thought thinking itself, then life thought otherwise than being present will consist in "a weak force" (V 13/xiv).[20] What is a weak force? A weak force is an ability to be unable. In other words, it is an ability based in an inability, an inability that can be made active and superlative, a force whose ante can be upped. As I shall show, the weak force is also double. Generally, however, the weak force will be a vulnerability that makes life unconditionally open to what comes: it receives. What I am trying to do is suggest an experiment in which unconditional nonhospitality is reversed into unconditional hospitality. Unconditional hospitality takes up the Kantian insight into the nature of the law; its form must be universal. The law must be applied equally or univocally to all. And yet, since unconditional hospitality is weak, this vulnerability refers to powerlessness (*impuissance*), to a lack, defect, or fault (*défaut* or *faute*) that results from no fall or decline (see CS11 192/132). The thought of this fault is at the center of Derrida's writings on animals; perhaps we have to say that it is at the center of his writings overall. It will therefore be my central concern here. In Derrida, this fault has many names; I shall consider several, starting with the *pharmakon*. The pharmakon is evil, and yet there is something good about it. Always in Derrida, the concern is with a logic of the limit—say, between evil and good—that is not oppositional, a logic in which the two poles are not external to one another. Always in Derrida, there is a search for the third genus, the third *genos*, the *Geschlecht* or *khōra*. The thought of the *khōra* in Derrida always implies a kind of thickening or multiplying of the limit, turning it into limit*s* (in the plural). But this new thought of the limit does not mean that I are going to reduce humans to being animals or elevate animals to human existence. I am not going to try to give language back to the animals. Instead, with Derrida, I am going to try to show, on the one hand, that *we* also are deprived of the phenomenological "as such" that defines essence and identity, we also suffer from this defect; and, on the other, I am going to try to understand the lack of speech, this silence, as something nonprivative, as something positive, even as something rational (A 74/ATIA 416). What I am going to do, following Derrida, is problematize what he calls "a worldwide anthropology [*une anthropologie mondiale*]" which is "a way for man today to posit himself over and against what he calls 'the animal' in what he calls 'the world'" (A 81).

The motifs of man, animal, and especially world must be problematized because it is precisely this absence in animals, this inability to speak and ask questions, this lack of access to the "as such," to the "as such" especially of death, that allows us, as human existence (*Dasein*), to treat them, animals, as scapegoats, to sacrifice them, to wage war on animals on a global scale. In his writings on animals, Derrida shows that no response to this "war of the species" is "sufficient." One response that is well known would be animal rights, that is, the extension of human rights to animals. While one must support, as I already pointed out, the actions of those who advocate animal rights, this idea does not avoid the risk of making the animal continuous with the human. In fact, the idea of rights in general does not avoid the worst, since it is based in the constitution of an unscathed sovereign subject. It is possible to argue that the notion of animal rights replicates the very violence it opposes. Is it possible to find a more sufficient response to the suffering of animals? Indeed, the most distant purpose of this book consists in the attempt to find a more sufficient response to this violence. As Derrida says in his dialogue with Roudinesco, "The relation between humans and animals *must* change" (DQD 108/64, Derrida's emphasis; cf.

CS11 160/106); a revolt is necessary (see DQD 112/67). As we can see already, such a revolt, which is really a decision, would be based on the generalization and the positivity of the fault. A central idea in this book is that the generalization of the fault will lead us to reconceive the difference between animals and humans as a "staggered analogy." The "staggered analogy" between animals and humans requires thought, but thought, I am going to claim, amounts to three things: waiting, following, and carrying. I must wait for what arrives—yet in the most desperate urgency; I must follow—yet without any program; I must carry you—yet or because the world has gone away. Here we must recall a line of poetry from Paul Celan, a line on which Derrida reflects in "Rams": "Die Welt fort, Ich muss dich tragen," "The world is gone, I must carry you." If the most distant aim of this book is to find a more sufficient response to the violence of our today, then the most pressing question is not, what is called thinking? but what is called carrying? I can make my leading question more precise: how is it possible to carry an animal who is singular? Is not the carrying of singularity precisely what is most impossible, because carrying (as in a meta-phor, a carrying over and beyond) desingularizes? In order to approach a response to the question of carrying, let us penetrate Derrida's diagnosis of our today as "a strange 'war' without war" (CS11 174/117).

ONE

War and Scapegoats

The Diagnosis: Globalization as War Without War

For Derrida, a today (or a date in general, an event) is never simple because repetition fundamentally determines all experience (A 44/ATIA 393). Derrida's thought always revolves around a kind of duplicity between a transcendental structure, which is relatively unchanging, and the appearance of that structure as an event (see MDA 96/92). Therefore he can say, on the one hand, that what is happening today "is as old as man, as old as what he calls his world, his knowledge, his history and his technology" (A 45/ATIA 393). Yet, on the other hand, he can claim that the event is very "new" and "unprecedented" (A 44/ATIA 393). Insofar as it is new and unprecedented, our today, for Derrida, seems to be "post-Kantian modernity" (V 118/80): the last two hundred years. Now, in his diagnosis of this very old and very new today that is ours, Derrida brings to light what he calls indices or signs. Here is the first sign, which concerns our relation to animals. In "The Animal that Therefore I Am," Derrida points out that our relation to animals is being transformed at a pace that is nearly impossible to calculate, and this transformation is due to the well-known advances in technology and forms of knowledge (A 44/ATIA 392). It is undeniable—and Derrida repeats this claim of undeniability frequently—that currently animals are being subjected to violence in the name of the well-being of man. But today's violence against animals goes well beyond the animal sacrifices recounted in the Bible and the texts of ancient Greece (A 45/ATIA 394). This is important, since I shall have a lot to say about sacrifice as I go forward. As I shall demonstrate, sacrifice itself must be sacrificed, and this sacrifice of sacrifice arises perhaps from one of the voices of Christianity.[1] But I am getting ahead of myself. What is happening today is worse than the ancient religious sacrifices of animals. Derrida even compares what is happening today to genocide and the Holocaust (see DQD 122/73): "[the annihilation of certain species] is occurring through the organization and exploitation of an artificial, infernal, virtually interminable survival, in conditions that previous generations would have found monstrous, outside of every supposed norm of a life proper to animals that are thus exterminated by means of their continued existence or even their overpopulation." We know what Derrida is speaking of: certain species are "farmed," making them more numerous and better fed, only in order to send them to "the same hell, that of the imposition of genetic experimentation or extermination by gas or fire" (A 46–46/ATIA 394–95; see also DQD 122/73).

As Derrida admits, these processes are all well known, and it is easy to conjure up the images of this violence. But then, and more important, Derrida turns to the pathos that these images of animal slaughter arouse in us: "If these images are 'pathetic,' if they evoke sympathy, it is also because they 'pathetically' open the immense question of pathos and the pathological, precisely, that is, of suffering, pity, and compassion; and the place that has to be accorded to the interpretation of this compassion, to the sharing of this suffering among the living, to the law, ethics, and politics that must be brought to bear upon this experience of compassion. For what has been happening now for two centuries involves a new experience of this compassion" (A 47/ ATIA 395).

As we know from his dialogue with Roudinesco, Derrida is sympathetic to those who speak of animal rights, even though he criticizes the concept of right (*droit*) (DQD 109/64, 112/67; FL 42–43/18–19). But here, in "The Animal that Therefore I am," he stresses that "these voices are raised" in order to awaken us precisely to this fundamental compassion. Indeed, no one can deny the suffering, the fear or panic, the terror or fright, as Derrida says, that humans witness in certain animals. The question of animals suffering leaves no doubt. Nevertheless, during the last two centuries, a war has been waged not only against animal life but also against this feeling of compassion. "War," Derrida says in conclusion, "is being waged over the subject of pity" (A 50/ ATIA 397). We can now see Derrida's diagnosis of our today, his "hypothesis," as he calls it:[2] the war between humans and animals is "passing through a critical phase" (A 50/ATIA 397). It is passing through a critical phase because animals are inside our communities, on our farms, and yet we think that their being in our communities does not require that we feel compassion for them. In this war, we are not required to have compassion for a part of ourselves. Instead, we can slaughter the animals fattened on our farms, so to speak, in us, in our subjectivity. We can see already the suicidal structure of the critical phase. But I am getting ahead of myself.

Complicating his dating of our today, and this is not the final complication we will see here, Derrida claims (this is based on *Rogues*, but this claim is quite explicit in *The "Concept" of September 11*)[3] that this critical phase really occurs after the end of the cold war (V 146/103). In general, post-Kantian modernity saw not only the acceleration of the compassionless technological treatment of animals; it also saw the rise of secularism. Yet, as Derrida says in *Rogues*, this secularization is "ambiguous"; even while it "frees itself from the religious . . . it remains marked, in its very concept, by the religious" (V 51/28). Therefore, at the end of the cold war, the religious returns. So, let's take up Derrida's 1994 essay "Faith and Knowledge," which provides more determination for the violence of today; it also opens up the question of, to use the English word again, "globalization." In "Faith and Knowledge," Derrida also speaks of "signs" of "today" (FS 48/35, paragraph 33; 53/38–39, paragraph 35). For Derrida, two things have to be explained in relation to the return of the religious today (FS 57–58/42–43, paragraph 37).

First, the return of the religious today is not a simple return; its globality and its figures (tele-techno-media-scientific, capitalistic, and politico-economic figures) remain original and unprecedented. But Derrida goes on: it is also not a *simple* return *of the religious*. The return involves a "radical destruction" of the religious, first, due to the war that fundamentalism wages against the Roman and state or organized churches and, second, due to a pacifist movement of universal fraternization, the reconciliation of "men, sons of the same God," these brothers basically all belonging to the monotheistic tradition of Abrahamic religions. Yet the movement of peace, according to Derrida, contains a double horizon. On the one hand, it involves the kenotic (or the emptying) horizon of the death of God and thus an anthropological reimmanentization. Here Derrida alludes to what the then-pope, John Paul II, said about the supreme value of human life. The pope's encyclicals seem to imply, Derrida suggests, that, after the death of the Christ, the first death of God, there will be a second death of God; the movement of peace would result in there being only man. No longer, in other words, would God be valued, but only man would be valued.[4] On the other hand, the pacifying movement involves a second horizon: the declaration of peace can also be a pacifying gesture, pacifying in the sense of subjugating. Referring to Rome, Derrida speaks of a kind of religious colonization, the imposition "surreptitiously [of] a discourse, a culture, a politics, and a right, to impose them on all the other monotheistic religions, including the non-Catholic Christian religions" (FS 57–58/43, paragraph 37). Beyond Europe, the aim would be to impose, in the name of peace, "a globalatinazation [*mondialatinasation*]" (FS 58/43, paragraph 37). For Derrida, who, like Foucault and Deleuze and Guattari,[5] reverses Clausewitz's famous saying ("War is politics by other means"), the movement of peace in the return of the religious is war "by other means": "the field of this war or this pacification is without limit" (FS 58/43, paragraph 37).

The second thing that needs to be explained provides more determination to the violence of this war. What needs to be explained, according to Derrida, is the autoimmune nature of the current return of the religious, secreting its own poison and its own antidote, its own *pharmakon*, we could say. The same movement that renders indissociable religion and tele-techno-scientific reason in its most critical aspect reacts inevitably to itself. As Derrida says, "It is the terrifying but fatal logic of the auto-immunity of the unscathed that will always associate science and religion" (FS 59/44, paragraph 37). Just as the processes of animal extermination are well known, how this autoimmunity works is well known. Quite simply, because global terrorism is indeed global, it would be impossible without the very technology (the cell phones, the e-mails, the jets of 9/11) that it is reacting against in the name of the unscathed nature of the religious (cf. CSII 154/101). But Derrida also points out that the use of this technology, this hyper-technology, is linked to what he calls "new archaic violence." The second nonhypertechnological violence resorts to "pre-machinal living being," "to bare hands," prehensile organs (for example, the cases of beheadings during the U.S. occupation of Iraq). In any case, Derrida summarizes the violence of the return of the religious in this way: "This archaic and ostensibly more savage radicalization of 'religious' violence claims, in the name of 'religion,' to allow the living community to rediscover its roots, its place, its body and its idiom intact (unscathed, safe, pure, proper). It spreads death and unleashes self-destruction in a desperate (auto-immune) gesture that attacks the blood of its own body: as though thereby to eradicate uprootedness and re-appropriate the sacredness of life safe and sound. Double root, double uprootedness, double eradication" (FS 71/53, paragraph 42). This quotation means that there is always violence, necessarily, at the root. This "archaic violence," this violence at the origin (*archē*) cannot be eliminated, even in the name of the archaic. I shall return to this originary or structural violence in a moment.[6]

It may seem as though, with the return of the religious today, we have left behind the question of the animal. But we have never left behind the question of the living. And, moreover, there is an explicit link between these two signs or indices: the Abrahamic religions are unified by the sacrifice of a ram, a substitute for the sacrifice of a man (FS 57/43, paragraph 37). As Derrida says in his dialogue with Jean-Luc Nancy, "Il faut bien manger": "The 'Thou shalt not kill'—with all its consequences, which are limitless—has never been understood within the Judeo-Christian tradition . . . as a 'Thou shalt not put to death the living in general.' This has become meaningful in religious cultures for which carnivorous sacrifice is essential, as being-flesh" (PS 293/279). Now we can start to see well that in which Derrida's diagnosis consists: after the end of the cold war, the religious accompanies, like a "shadow" (FS 58/44, paragraph 37), globalization, but *globalization is war "by other means."* Even more, the violence of this war, which is violence against the living in general, is autoimmune precisely because it is global and therefore limitless.

Derrida, however, presents his diagnosis of the post–cold war "today" in *Rogues*. Here we encounter another complication of the dating of our "today." In *Rogues*, Derrida tells us that over the last two hundred years the idea of democracy has come to be no longer restricted to intranational constitutions; instead, it is now international, that is, it determines the relations among nations. But it is important that Derrida, in *Rogues* (but *Rogues* is not the only place; we should look at *Politics of Friendship* and "Force of Law," too), analyzes texts that date from between the two world wars: Husserl's *The Crisis of European Science*, which dates from 1935; Benjamin's *The Critique of Violence*, which dates from 1921, and Schmitt's *The Concept of the Political*, which dates from 1932. It seems to me that Derrida focuses on this period, the time between the two world wars, because a world war is *already* a form of globalization; it announces globalization. Because a world war encompasses the whole world, and because, in order to encompass the whole world, it must rely on technoscience, the attack in a world war can come from anywhere and at a distance (long-range missiles launched at sea, for example); in a world war, already, it is becoming increasingly difficult to identify the enemy (see PA 278/248; CS11 154/101, 164/109). Nevertheless, as Derrida points out, the world wars were fought between sovereign nation-state unities or between coalitions of nation-state unities; then, we could still, for the most part, identify the enemy (and note the general name here, "the enemy," which resembles the general name "the animal").

Today, however, after the end of the cold war, the fragility of the nation-state is being tested more and more, and the denials of its fragility, according to Derrida, are manifestations that the state is in its death throes. Agencies such as the International Criminal Court and the demand for universal human rights encroach on nation-state sovereignty. But the result of this universalization or "worldwide-ization" is that the concept of war, and thus of world war, of enemy, and even of terrorism, along with the distinctions between civilian and military or among army, police, and militia—all these concepts and distinctions are losing their pertinence (V 212/154, 150/106). As Derrida says in *Rogues* and in *The "Concept" of September 11*, what is "called September 11 will not have created or revealed this situation, although it will have surely media-theatricalized it" (V 212/154–55; CS11 163/108). According to Derrida in *Rogues*, this is the situation we have inherited from the end of the cold war. The context consists in "the so-called globalization [*mondialisation*]" being "more in-egalitarian and violent than ever, therefore, more alleged and less worldwide than ever. . . . There is no *the* [Derrida's emphasis] world [*il n'y a pas* le *monde*]" (V 213/155, translation modified; see also CS11 179/121).[7] In this quotation (as I noted), Derrida italicizes the definite article, "il n'y a pas *le* monde." In our so-called *mondialisation*, the world seems more restricted than ever, "smaller than ever," as we say popularly. The world is no longer *the* world because the world no longer functions as "a backdrop" (*un fond*, as Derrida says) for human endeavors (let us say quickly, for capitalism). With so-called globalization, it is as if we are not in the world, but the world is in us; or, more precisely, as Derrida says, the world is concentrated into a small "parcel," the Latin parcel, which is also English or even American: "the United States and its allies." The part encircles the whole like a sphere. This sphericity of the enclosure of the world explains Derrida's suspicions concerning the word "globalization" that we use in the Anglophone world (CS11 179–121).[8] This enclosure means that "*mondialisation* is not taking place" (CS11 181/123). If "worlding" is not taking place, then a declosing is required.

To be clear, let me add here that this comment that there is no *the* world does not mean that we are abandoning Heidegger's now-classical formula of being-in-the-world. What we are doing, following Derrida, but also Deleuze, is rethinking the relation expressed by this formula. The relation is based on temporal ecstasies or temporalization. In the experience of temporalization, which is autoaffection, as I shall discuss in chapter 2, the world goes away in two senses. On the one hand, the second world of Platonism goes away (is *fort*), which leaves only this world. To put this idea very simply, Heidegger, of course, is not Platonistic in the sense of a two-world schema. This reduction of the two worlds into one cannot be avoided. There is no the world in the sense, then, of a world in itself, no essential world behind the appearance. There is only a bottomlessness, an abyss. Yet the world goes away in a second sense. In globalization, the world is reduced to the sphere of human endeavors; it is reduced to the parcel of the West, "the United States and its allies." The world goes away in the sense of the world being reduced to an enclosure of extended space. This extension requires a declosing.[9] When the declosing happens, there is (instead of globalization) mondialization. We must make a terminological distinction (one that Derrida himself never makes, as far as I know) between "globalization:" and "mondialization," between, I would say to anticipate, "enclosure" and "spacing" (*espacement*). When Derrida says in *The "Concept" of September 11* that "*mondialisation* is not taking place," he means that spacing is not taking place. Spacing *must* happen in order to institute not a war without war but a peace without peace.

At the end of the cold war, what we have is precisely a "war without war"; there are still clashes of forces. In the clashes that take place in this so-called globalization, there is no identifiable enemy in the form of a state territory with which the encircling part ("the United States and its allies") would wage what could still be called a war, even if we think of this as a war on international terrorism (cf. CS11 144/94). The balance of terror of the cold war that ensured that no escalation of nuclear weapons would lead to a suicidal operation, Derrida says, "all that is over" (V 214/156; cf. CS11 144/94). Instead, "a new violence is being prepared and in truth has been unleashed for some time now, in a way that is more visibly suicidal or auto-immune than ever. This violence no longer has to do with *world* war or even with *war*, even less with some right to wage war. And this is hardly reassuring—indeed, quite the contrary" (V 215/156; cf. PA 302/272, CS11 145/94). Let me repeat this crucial comment: "A new violence is being prepared and in truth has been unleashed for some time now, in a way that is more visibly suicidal [*plus visiblement suicidaire*] or auto-immune than ever." What does it mean to be "more suicidal"?

To be more suicidal is to kill oneself *more*. But, again, and in slightly other terms, how can one kill *more* of oneself? The "more" that I have stressed means that, since there is only a fragile distinction between states (there is no identification of the enemy), one's state or self includes more and more of the others (we could take up the problem of immigration here). But, if one's self includes others that threaten (so-called terrorist cells, for example [cf. CS11 146/95]), then one must murder more and more of those others that are inside in order to immunize oneself. Since the others are *inside* oneself, one is required to kill more and more of oneself. This context is very different from the rigid and external opposition, symbolized by the so-called iron curtain, that defined the cold war. There and then, "we" had an identifiable enemy, with a name, which allowed the number of the enemies to be limited. But here and now, today, the number of enemies—*all of us*, we might say, are rogues—is unlimited. Every other is wholly other ("*tout* autre est tout autre" [PA 259/232]), and thus every single other needs to be rejected by the immune system. This innumerable rejection resembles a genocide or, what is worse, an absolute threat. During the cold war, the absolute threat of a nuclear war was contained by game theory (which refers to calculative reason). Derrida says, however, in the first essay of *Rogues*, "The Reason of the Strongest," that

> [the absolute threat] can no longer be contained when it comes neither from an already constituted state nor even from a potential state that might be treated as a rogue state. Such a situation rendered futile or ineffective all the rhetorical resources (not to mention military resources) spent on justifying the word *war* and the thesis that the "war against international terrorism" had to target particular states that give financial backing or logistical support or provide a safe haven for terrorism, states that, as it is said in the United States, "sponsor" or "harbor" terrorists. All these efforts to identify "terrorist" states or rogue states are "rationalizations" aimed *not* at denying so much some absolute anxiety but the panic or terror before the fact that the absolute threat no longer comes from or is under the control of some state or some identifiable state form.   (V 149/105; cf. CS11 150–151/98)

This comment should make us reflect on the recent rhetoric in the United States about Iran and North Korea; the rhetoric is *probably* a rationalization to make us think that we have reentered a kind of cold war, while the real threat comes from agencies that may have nuclear weapons and are not defined by national borders. In any case, what Derrida is saying here is that the worst is possible, here and now, *more possible than ever*. The worst threat is an event still to come (V 148/104; cf. CS11 149/97).

Following Derrida, I have been analyzing the event (still to come) of the worst. But the worst also has a structure.[10] The worst, a superlative, is the most suicidal, the most autoimmune, since in the name of purity it threatens to contaminate everything, in the name of life it threatens to kill everything, "le tout." The structure of the worst is a question of numbers, and it calls for a rationality that is more than calculative. In "Faith and Knowledge" (paragraph 50, almost at the end of the essay, FS 85–86/65), Derrida says, "But the more than One [*le plus d'Un*] is without delay more than two. There is no alliance of two unless it is to signify in effect the pure madness of pure faith. The worst violence. The more than One is this n + One which introduces the order of faith or of trust in the address of the other, but also the mechanical, machine-like division (testimonial affirmation and reactivity, 'yes, yes,' etc., remote-control murder, ordered at a distance even when it rapes and kills with bare hands). The possibility of radical evil both destroys and institutes the religious." This ambiguous phrase "le plus d'un" could be translated in English as "more of one" or "no more one" or "more than one." On the one hand, this phrase means that in autoaffection, even while it is "auto," the same, there is more than one; immediately with one, there is no more one (n + 1 becomes n−1),[11] there is a division into two, a kind of fault line between the self and other(s). On the other hand, the phrase means that there is a lot more of one, only one, the most one. The worst derives from this second sense of "plus d'un." In this crucial passage, Derrida is making a distinction between the worst (evil) and radical evil (see also FL 61/28). As for Kant, for Derrida, radical evil is literally radical, evil at the root; it is entwined with humanity and is inextirpable by human powers; it is evil in the heart.[12] For Derrida, radical evil consists in the inconceivable, small, "infinitesimal difference" (*une différence infime* [DLG 333/234]) that precedes and makes possible a me and an other, that precedes and makes possible a me and an other in me. Derrida would describe this infinitesimal hiatus (*un écart infime*) as the address, the "à" or the "to"; it is not only difference, across the distance of the address; it is also repetition. And it is not only a repetition; this self-divergence is also violence, a rending of one- self, an incision. Here we must pause and recognize that, if the self-relation or autoaffection always, necessarily, includes this in- finitesimal violence, if thought is violence to an other as to itself, then the principal content of thought is violence and therefore in- justice. The question of peace and justice, in a word, deconstruc- tion, arises only on the basis of this new conception of thought.[13] Then there is no greater call to thinking than violence. And if we are not thinking of violence, we are still not thinking.

Nevertheless, thought as violence, radical evil, is not absolute evil (CS11 151/99). The worst violence occurs—we have to won- der here if the worst is really possible or is it the impossible it- self—when the other to which one is related is completely ap- propriated to or completely in one's self, when an address reaches its proper destination, when it reaches only its proper destina- tion. Reaching only its proper destination, the address will ex- clude more, many more, and that "many more," at the limit, amounts to all. It is this complete exclusion or this extermina- tion of the most—there is no limit to this violence (CS11 151/99)—that makes this violence the worst violence. The worst is a relation that makes of more than one simply one, that makes, out of a division, an indivisible sovereignty. The worst is not the opposite of Leibniz's best possible world. We must recognize that the worst is not the worst world; it is the end of the world, no world, no future, total apocalypse. The worst is, as Deleuze and Guattari say in *A Thousand Plateaus*, "the suicidal state," "realized nihilism," in a word, fascism,[14] Or, as Foucault says at the end of *The History of Sexuality*, when power becomes biopower, when war becomes a concern of populations, then wars "have never been so bloody."[15] In its most paradoxical formula, the worst vio- lence would be a violence that produced something absolutely alive and absolutely dead (VP 115/102). It would be dead because its actual life would exclude—kill—all virtualities or potentialities. In this formula, we can see that the worst resembles the "pure actuality," the *energeia*, of Aristotle's Prime Mover, the One God: the sphere or, better, the *globe* of thought thinking itself and only itself (V 35/15). The religious always accompanies this process like a shadow. Or, to put this paradoxical idea of the worst in another way, absolute life would be absolute spirit, and absolute spirit, being spiritual, would be dead, absolutely dead. Through the worst, we have returned to the two "ends of man": life and death in spirit or of spirit. We must keep in mind that, at least according to Heidegger, spirit is required for there to be evil.

The Risks Involved in Attacking the "Anthropological Limit": Biological Continuism and Metaphysical Separationism

To stop the worst, we must keep these two ends of man together (but not gathered together). In other words, if this structure truly defines the worst, then what is required, here and now, in the age of so-called globalization, is a lesser violence, "violence against violence" (ED 173/11): as Derrida says as early as "Violence and Metaphysics," "the least possible violence" (ED 191/130). The lesser violence would be a limited violence, and therefore, as anticipated, a new logic of the limit is required, a new logic of the limit that would keep the future open (CS11 169/113). This logic of the limit will problematize what Derrida in *Aporias* calls "the anthropological limit" (AP 77/41). In other words, it will problematize the absolute oppositional limit between the living being called man and the living being called animal (GL 37–38/27). In "The Animal that Therefore I Am," Derrida, on the one hand, speaks of "thickening" (*épaissir*) the limit, of "multiplying [*multiplier*] and increasing" it, that is, he wants to try to make the limit more and more divisible; this multiplication of the limit provides one reason for Derrida's insistence on the plural "les animaux" (A 51/ATIA 398). (As I shall discuss, there is another and more important reason for this insistence on the plural.) On the other hand, however, this multiplication does not mean that we are going to give to animals the property of which man says they are deprived. Instead, the property by means of which man separates himself from animals (like a separate substance) has to be "ratcheted down" (*démultiplier*) (A 219). As I shall show, man, too, is deprived of this property, the "as such." In this new logic of the limit, the question is: what does a limit become once it is abyssal, once the frontier no longer forms a single *in*divisible line but more than one internally divided line, once consequently it can no longer be traced, objectified, or counted as single and indivisible (A 53/ATIA 399)?

Derrida is not attacking this exterior or absolute oppositional limit frontally. But any attack, even an oblique attack, involves certain risks; indeed, to avoid or at least negotiate with these risks provides the only means to determine something like a sufficient response to the violence humans wage against animals. Here are the risks. On the one hand, an attack on the anthropological limit could amount to reducing the human down to the animal, down to the biological, down to irrational instincts and forces. In other words, the limit between man and animals could become one of homogeneous continuity; we could have a biological continuism (A 52/ATIA 398) or, even more simply, biologism. For instance, biologism would say that there is no difference at all between a reaction to a stimulus and a response to a question (see A 172–173/128).[16] This risk of biologism is really the risk of a direct attack on the difference between animals and humans. If one raises animals to the level of humans, or if one lowers humans to the level of animals, one ignores the difference that requires living beings to be treated in a variety of ways. With a direct approach, either humans are going to be treated like animals or animals like humans. An oblique attack, in contrast, keeps open the possibility of different treatments. With continuism, one produces a result that is, as Derrida says, making a wordplay, "simply too asinine," "simplement trop bête" (A 52/ ATIA 398). Then, because of the problems with continuism, one could go in the opposite direction and make the limit between the human and the animal once again oppositional.[17] One could then institute a metaphysical separation between two substances, between man and animal. For Derrida, when Heidegger in "The Self-assertion of the German University" speaks of a spiritual world as the power that preserves a people's force ("*Macht*" and "*Kraft*," of course, in Heidegger's German; "*puissance*" and "*force*" in the French translation), connected as that force is to the earth and blood,[18] Heidegger exemplifies the complicity of these two risks, a biological continuism and an oppositional separation. In *Of Spirit* (which dates from 1987), Derrida asks, what is the price of Heidegger's strategy here? On the one hand, Derrida thinks that Heidegger's spiritualization of biological force implies that he does not demarcate himself from biologism. On the other, because he does not demarcate himself clearly from biologism, he then in turn opposes biologism only "by re-inscribing spirit in an oppositional determination, by once again making it a unilaterality of subjectivity, even if in its voluntarist form" (DLE 65/39). Heidegger's strategy results in the worst; it capitalizes on both the risks or on both the evils: by not demarcating itself off, it ends up sanctioning Nazism, or, more generally, racism, by spiritualizing it, and when it demarcates itself off, it ends up, through spirit, making a gesture that is still metaphysical. Derrida claims, in *Of Spirit*, that it is urgent to find the least bad (less worse) form of complicity with the biologistic and the metaphysical risks (DLE 66/40). The new logic of the limit is supposed to be a response to this urgency of the least bad or the less worse.

With this new logic of the limit, Derrida is still speaking of the logic of autoimmunity. In the interview called *The "Concept" of September 11*—but I anticipated this claim earlier—Derrida tells us that "the *pharmakon* is another name, an old name, for this auto-immunity logic" (CS11 182/124). If we are to pursue this new logic, then it seems that we are required to return to Derrida's early essay "Plato's Pharmacy." We must understand the logic of the pharmakon if we are to understand the logic of autoimmunity. To anticipate, two features define both logics: there is no propriety, and there is no indivisibility or gathering. But we can see another reason for returning to this early essay. In "Plato's Pharmacy," Derrida compares the pharmakon to democracy as Plato describes it in book 8 of the *Republic*, and in this context he uses the term *"voyou"* (DIS 165/143).[19] In *Rogues*, Plato's idea of a republic, with its sovereign philosopher, is always in question (see especially V 55/31–32).[20] But we can find one more motivation, and perhaps this is the most important. If we are going to reconceive the limit between man and animal, then we are rethinking the limit between two genera, a rethinking that requires a third genus, which would be the *khōra*. "Plato's Pharmacy" is the first time in which Derrida speaks of the *khōra*. Therefore, if, following Derrida, we are to rethink the anthropological limit, then we must rethink the problem of the animal all the way down into its "soil" (*sol*) and all the way down into the "base of the column" (*socle*) that keeps the institution of this limit erect (cf. A 50/397). In the briefest terms, that pursuit means a kind of return to the Greeks. Or more precisely, and I do not think this is an exaggeration, our today remains bound up with the project of reversing Platonism.

Scapegoats

Published in 1968, "Plato's Pharmacy" belongs to the moment of anti-Platonism. Therefore "Plato's Pharmacy" belongs to a set of texts produced at the same moment by other members of Derrida's generation: Deleuze's 1965 "Reversing Platonism" and Foucault's 1968 "This Is Not a Pipe."[21] The logic of anti-Platonism is well known, but let us recall some of its features. Since Nietzsche, anti-Platonism is the attempt to reverse, as Deleuze's title suggests, hierarchies set up in Plato's philosophy, hierarchies that are then appropriated into the metaphysical tradition: the hierarchies between the invisible or intelligible and the visible or sensible; between the soul and body; between living memory and rote memory; between *mnēmē* and *hypomnēsis*; between voice and writing; between, finally, good and evil. Reversing hierarchies means that anti-Platonism is always concerned with values, a concern that privileges, out of the series of hierarchies, the one between good and evil. What was previously evil, this world, is now good, and vice versa. But reversing the hierarchies also means that one eliminates the oppositional or juxtaposed relation between the two poles of the hierarchy. The true world, in other words, must be reduced to this one; dualisms must be reduced. This reduction is a reduction to immanence. Although this term makes us think immediately of Deleuze, Derrida uses the term, albeit in scare quotes, in "Plato's Pharmacy" (DIS 111/98; see also DIS 11/6; TJLN 334/298).[22] In any case, the central idea is that the second or intelligible world is now immanent to *this* world. But, on the basis of this reversal and reduction, we can see retrospectively that a decision (a perhaps impossible decision) instituted the hierarchy and made the separation in the first place. This decision is Platonism. There is, however, a second step in the reversal-reduction of Platonism. If we want to "twist free" of Platonism—to use Heidegger's phrase (*herausdrehen*)[23]—we must find a difference within immanence, not only a difference that is nondualistic but also a difference that destabilizes the original decision. In other words, we must find a difference of forces that is, as Derrida would say, undecidable.

If one knows a bit about deconstruction (or Nietzscheanism), the structure of reversal, undecidability, and decision is obvious.[24] Yet this structure (which is opposed to the worst) is crucial to what I am doing here. The worst values one living being, let us say, man, as the one and only good; everything else—more and more, the number keeps growing—is evil. In the reversal, and here I am trying to be more precise, what happens is a generalization of evil to all living beings. Evil is shared; power is abused by all living beings. If all living beings are evil (none of them is perfect like machines), then all of them—every single one of them, including me—are eligible for forgiveness. But the generalization of evil has the additional effect of making the valuation indeterminate. If all of them are evil, it is not certain, I cannot be certain, that this one is more evil than the other one. Perhaps the most evil is most deserving of forgiveness. This "perhaps" is the experience of the undecidable. Yet a decision is required here and now because there are conditions. The conditions are a fact. It is not possible to grant forgiveness unconditionally to every single living being. All living beings, including me, we might say, are "pharmakons," and I must decide, here and now, which one or ones will be made welcome, will be revalued as remedies. A difference must be made, but one that will be always insufficient since there are always more who are worthy of forgiveness.

I am here anticipating the overall direction of the thinking in which I am engaged. But having introduced the term "pharmakon," I may circle back to "Plato's Pharmacy." In the interview *Positions* and in the preface to *Dissemination*, Derrida identifies the reversal of such hierarchies as one of deconstruction's two phases (POS 56–58/41–42; DIS 10–12/4–6). The second phase reinscribes the previously inferior term as the "origin" or "resource" of the hierarchy itself. In this second phase, deconstruction eliminates the external oppositions. Making use of the previously inferior term to refer to the resource, this name becomes what Derrida calls an "old name" or a "paleonym." In *Positions*, Derrida provides a list of these "old terms," one of which is "pharmakon" (POS 58–59/43). I think it is safe to say that all these terms refer, for Derrida, to the experience of a process of differentiation that is also repetition, or, to put this idea more simply, the terms refer to the experience of language where language is taken in a broad sense. So, in "Plato's Pharmacy," "pharmakon" refers to the resource called the *logos*, language, but language prior to its division between living voice and dead writing. In other words, and Derrida says that this is "the single theme of the essay," the pharmakon is the "indissociability" of the signifier and the signified concept (DIS 113/100; here, of course, Derrida uses the language of structuralism so much in vogue at this time). The pharmakon then refers to language prior to the decision to separate and make determinate the signified concept or form from the sensible body of language; it refers to language prior to the decision to value the form more than the matter. The pharmakon is therefore prior to the decision that institutes Platonism or metaphysics.[25]

Insofar as the pharmakon consists in all the powers of repetition, it is, as Derrida says in "Plato's Pharmacy," an "element" (DIS 101/89). In regard to this element, we must recall what Heidegger says in "The Letter on Humanism": "Being, as the *element* [*das Element*] of thinking, is abandoned by the technical interpretation of thinking. . . . Thinking is [then] judged by a standard that does not measure up to it. Such judgment may be compared to the procedure of trying to evaluate the essence and power of a fish by seeing how long it can *live* [*leben*] on dry land."[26] Like Heidegger, Derrida gives us the figure of the *logos* as a liquid. But, unlike Heidegger, Derrida does not put the technological outside of the element; he does not put the threat or, more generally, death external to life. Derrida says, "in liquids, opposites more easily pass into one another. Liquid is the element of the *pharmakon*. And water, pure liquidity, lets itself be most easily and dangerously penetrated then corrupted by the *pharmakon*, with which it mixes [*mélange*] and immediately composes" (DIS 175/152). Through the verb "to mix"— "*mélanger*" here—we can see that, in "Plato's Pharmacy," in Derrida in general, there is a kind of "mixturism."[27] But what kind? It is possible to conceive mixture, and Derrida thinks that this conception can be found in Plato's *Philebus* (DIS 146/128), as an impure mixture, that is, as a mixture of two elements that were previously heterogeneous to one another and therefore were previously pure (DIS 146/128). The pharmakon in contrast is neither a simple, noncomposite element nor a composite of previously separate or clear-cut elements that are opposed to one another (DIS 144–145/126–127). The pharmakon is *not* a medium (here Derrida uses the word "*milieu*," which means literally "a halfway place") in which prior pure elements come to be mixed; it is not a mixture that is second; it is also not the simplicity of a *coincidentia oppositorum* (DIS 146/127, 105/93) or an "undifferentiated generality" (DIS 149/130).[28] Being prior to all oppositions and purifying separations, the pharmakon is an "element-medium," which means that the *milieu* is itself the prior element. In the pharmakon, what we have is "absolutely heterogeneous elements" that nevertheless "compose" (DIS 111/98; cf. TJLN 144–45/125–126). It is important to recognize here that what Derrida is calling the pharmakon is *not* a relationship of equiprimordiality (*Gleichursprünglichkeit*), as Heidegger would say, but a relationship of "origin-heterogeneous," as Derrida himself says in *Of Spirit* (DLE 177/107–108).[29] Origin-heterogeneous defines all Derrida's best-known "old names," including, of course, "différance" (see DIS 146/127).

But Derrida repeatedly calls the pharmakon "ambivalent" (DIS 144–145/126–127); we must take this word literally— ambivalent, two values (at the least)—since what is at issue in "Plato's Pharmacy" is the possibility of value positing. As the myth that Socrates recounts in the second half of the *Phaedrus* indicates, the king will determine the value of writing or the pharmakon in the act of receiving; he will institute or constitute the value of the pharmakon, which will have no value in itself (DIS 85/76). In the chapter that is simply called "The Pharmakon" (chapter 4), Derrida stresses that the word "pharmakon" could be translated either as "remedy" (which is the traditional translation) or as "poison," or as both remedy and poison (DIS 111/98): the pharmakon is, at once, good and evil (DIS 160/139). Insofar as the pharmakon poisons, it interrupts; insofar as it heals, it communicates. The value of two forces, then—two forces that are always composed together—is at stake here, the force of communication and the force of interruption (DIS 111/98), the force of imprinting and the force of erasing. The idea of impressions is why, throughout "Plato's Pharmacy," Derrida stresses the Greek word "*typoi*," "types," as in the typewriter; it also explains why he stresses that the Greek word for "elements" is "*stoikeia*," "letters," as in letters of the alphabet (DIS 134/159). Of course, in this context, speaking of *stoikeia*, Derrida mentions the *khōra*, the receptacle, like wax, for the impression of forms (see also CNPP 582/50). Nevertheless, the pharmakon, through the force of interruption, always includes the possibility of destroying the communication. This threatening possibility included in the pharmakon is why the pharmakon is always "caught" (*pris*), as Derrida says, in the mixture of Platonism (DIS 112/99).[30] The verb "*prendre*," "to take," is, for Derrida, the verb of contamination (VP 20/20; cf. MLA 79/46; in

"Plato's Pharmacy," Derrida speaks of contamination on DIS 124/109, for example). The verb "to take," of course, suggests the hand, and we can see this, when Derrida speaks of the pharmakon being "apprehended," as in "prehensile," by Platonism (DIS 146/128). The grasping by the hand makes the communication (or play) "stop" (*s'arrêter*) (DIS 146/127, 146/128). As Derrida says, "the opposition between *mnēmē* and *hypomnēsis* would thus preside over the meaning of writing. This opposition will appear to us to form a system with all the great structural oppositions of Platonism. What is played out at the limit between these two concepts is consequently something like the major decision of philosophy, the one through which it institutes itself, maintains itself, and contains its adverse foundation [*fond*]" (DIS 126/111). The decision, however, really concerns the attempt to separate the good pharmakon from its evil twin, a separation that allows the good pharmakon to be restored.

In "Plato's Pharmacy," Derrida gives us a striking example through which we can think about this decision. Here we return not only to the logic of autoimmunity but also to the question of sacrifice, to the question of animality. We could even say that here we anticipate Derrida's work on the death penalty (DQD 239/147). In the network of terms in ancient Greek associated with the term "pharmakon," there is the term "pharmakos," which means "wizard," "magician," or "poisoner" (DIS 146/128). Although Plato never uses this term, as far as Derrida knows—Plato uses a synonym of it, "*pharmakeus*"—Derrida feels justified to include it in his interpretation of the *Phaedrus* because there are "hidden forces of attraction" between a word that is present in Plato's text and words that are absent (DIS 149/130).[31] What Derrida is interested in is that "some have compared the character of the *pharmakos* to a scapegoat [*un bouc émissaire*]" (DIS 149/130).[32] We might say here "a ram." In any case, in ancient Greece, the ritual of *pharmakos* occurred when a city was suffering from some evil like a plague. A designated person or persons were taken outside the city walls; they were then beaten to drive the evil out of their bodies in order to achieve purification not just for their bodies but also and more importantly for the body of the city. In one of the texts Derrida cites, the *pharmakoi* are called "a sacrifice" (DIS 152/133). The logic of the *pharmakos* works in this way. The city's own or proper body is restored "by violently excluding from its territory the representative of an external threat." So, the *pharmakos* represented "the otherness of evil that comes . . . to infect the inside by unpredictably breaking into it." But then we get the twist: "the representative of the outside is nonetheless constituted, regularly granted its place by the community, chosen, kept, fed, etc., in the very heart of the inside"; Derrida continues, "these parasites were as a matter of course domesticated by the living organism that housed them at its expense" (DIS 152/133). In other words, they are part of the city's own body just as cats and dogs are. But this participation in and expulsion from the city's own body mean that the ceremony of the *pharmakos* is played out at the limit between inside and outside; the *pharmakos* himself represents evil both introjected and projected. In a crisis such as a plague, the passage to a decision about good and evil would attempt to undo the "conjunction" (DIS 153/133). And yet, because the ancient Greeks knew that the threat of a crisis comes without warning, in surprise, they prepared for it by fixing a regular date for the sacrifice. As Derrida notes, the date for the annual ceremony in ancient Greece was the same as Socrates' birthday (DIS 153/134). As I shall discuss in chapter 3, this question of the date, its regularity and singularity, is crucial.

The need to repeat the decision indicates that the *pharmakos* or, more precisely the pharmakon "constitutes the original milieu of that decision, the element that precedes it, comprehends it, goes beyond it, can never be reduced to it, and is not separated from it by a single word" (DIS 112/99). Indeed, Derrida says that the pharmakon is the *milieu* prior to any possible dissociation of opposites, even the opposites of form and content or form and matter. This "priority," which Derrida puts in scare quotes, means that the pharmakon is formless like wax (DIS 119/104, 172/149), like Descartes's piece of wax. Undoubtedly, one of Derrida's central projects is to rethink extension in the Cartesian sense as *espacement*, as spacing (CNPP 568/37); this project leads Derrida to the *khōra*—but I am getting ahead of myself (CNPP 585/54). Nevertheless, through *espacement*, the *khōra* and the pharmakon are connected. The pharmakon is, then, not just a place, *un mi-lieu*, it is "atopos" (DIS 180/156) or a "non-lieu" (K 55/107), or even "la place du mort," literally "the place of the dead" (DIS 104/92). It is the blind spot (cf. DIS 154/135, 193/166). The blindness caused by the pharmakon, a kind of weakness or fault of vision, amounts to the only way, it seems to me, to twist free of Platonism. Here we could turn to a lengthy discussion of Heidegger's interpretation of Nietzsche's idea of life as the will to power and to Foucault's idea of modern biopower; it can be shown that these two ideas, will to power and biopower, are virtually identical.[33] Yet only the blindness that Derrida describes throughout his career, but especially, I think, in *Memories of the Blind*, opens up what we might call "points of resistance" to this form of power. This blindness destabilizes all hierarchies, all evaluations, all decisions, all limits. In short, values cannot be properly posited or juxtaposed. Because of this fundamental blindness, one cannot determine whether what is looking at you is a remedy or a poison, a menace or a benefit, a human or an animal. There is only uncertainty, which tests one and makes one suffer. Lacking the identification (the name) that would separate one from the other, one cannot sacrifice the scapegoat without feeling guilty, without feeling compassion. An evaluation therefore is never sufficient. This lack of vision, this "just to see" (cf. A 19/ATIA 373), then necessitates that we decide everything again.

Conclusion: In Poverty

As I said, I do not think that it is an exaggeration to say that our today remains bound up with the project of reversing Platonism. One very clear sign of anti-Platonism is the reductionistic project of naturalism in contemporary analytic philosophy; most generally, naturalism attempts to explain everything by means of what the natural sciences tell us about this world down here.[34] But there is a clear sign of anti-Platonism from Derrida, too. In the dialogue in *The "Concept" of September 11*, which took place in 2001, Derrida says, "Even if this 'in the name of' [democracy] is still merely an assertion and a purely verbal commitment. Even in its most cynical mode, such an assertion still lets resonate within it an invincible promise. I don't," he says, "hear any such promise coming from 'bin Laden' [Derrida puts this name in scare quotes to indicate its metonymic status; it stands not solely for the individual but also for a whole network of ideas and institutions], at least not for *this world* [*ce monde-ci*]" (CS11 169/114; Derrida's emphasis). I would have translated "ce monde-ci" as "this world down here," which more clearly indicates immanence. Yet, as in Nietzsche, every form of anti-Platonism ends up privileging immanence *as life*. If we stop here, however, with naturalism or vitalism—naturalism always brings along the risk of reducing reason to calculation (see V 186/133)—we have not really twisted free from Platonism. To do that, it is necessary that life never be simple life or simple nature; it must be "life without life" (D 119/88).[35] Consider two comments that, I think, are indicative of Derrida's attempt to move beyond simple life. The first comes from "Force of Law" (in 1989); there, speaking of Benjamin, Derrida says, "he [that is, Benjamin] stands up vigorously against all sacralization of life *for itself*, natural life, the simple fact of life" (FL 125/53; Derrida's emphasis). The second comment was written twenty years earlier, in "Freud and the Scene of Writing" (in 1966): "Life must be thought of as *trace* before being may be determined as presence" (ED 302/203; my emphasis).

We can see this same criticism of simple life in "Plato's Pharmacy." As I have noted, the *logos*, which is the pharmakon itself, is composed of written traces or "*typoi*," the imprints; these mechanical repetitions are "external or alien" to the life of memory; the traces come "from the outside" of the *psyche* and of *physis* (DIS 115/102): "the written traces," Derrida says, "no longer even belong to the order of the *physis*, since they are not alive" (DIS 119/104–105). The trace or the pharmakon is so hostile to natural life that it goes against "not only life unaffected by any illness, but even sick life, or rather the life of the sickness" (DIS 113/100). The pharmakon, then, for Derrida, is "the enemy of the living in general, whether healthy or sick" (DIS 113/100). In fact, the pharmakon, which as remedy is supposed to produce the positive and eliminate the negative, displaces and at the same time multiplies the effects of the negative, "leading the lack that was its cause to proliferate" (DIA 113/100). In other words, normal or natural disease defends itself from the pharmaceutical aggression, multiplying and reinforcing "the points of resistance" (DIS 115/101). But we must not be mistaken here. For Derrida, the pharmakon, insofar as it is mechanical repetition, is external only to natural or simple life: "the living being is finite (and its malady as well) . . . death is already inscribed and prescribed *within* [*dans*] its structure" (DIS 115/101). Death is in life, and here we must no longer speak of any sort of naturalism or biologism but perhaps a "mortalism."[36]

But we can go one step further. In "Plato's Pharmacy," Derrida entertains the possibility that writing, the trace, or the pharmakon might belong to nature. But then he says, if it does, "wouldn't it [belong] to that moment of the *physis*, to that necessary movement through which its truth, the production of its appearing, tends, says Heraclitus, to take shelter in its crypt" (DIS 119/105). The pharmakon, in other words, would belong to that moment of nature that loves to hide. Hiding, the pharmakon would never be able to appear as an essence or *eidos* (DIS 144/126); it would never be able to appear in truth, naked, or "as such" (DIS 181/157). I must stress in passing that this interpretation of Heraclitus's fragment, this interpretation of hiding, which implies a privation (*steresis*), already puts Derrida's thought in confrontation with Heidegger's: in the "Physis" lecture, Heidegger interprets *steresis* in terms of "the simplicity of essence" (*die Einfalt ihres Wesens*).[37] But, with Derrida, to say this again, the pharmakon never appears simply and never appears as essence. Thus the pharmakon does not respond to questions, and it is not responsible (DIS 156/136). As Derrida says (here speaking of imitation), the pharmakon "does not correspond to its essence, is not what it is . . . unless it is in some way at fault [*fautive*] or rather in default [*en défaut*]. It is bad by essence. It is good only insofar as it is bad. Since failure [*faillite*: failure of a business enterprise] is inscribed within it, it has no nature; nothing is properly its own" (DIS 160/139, cf. V 154/109). The pharmakon, in other words, is always in poverty, miserable, and therefore in need of compassion.

TWO

Animals Have No Hand

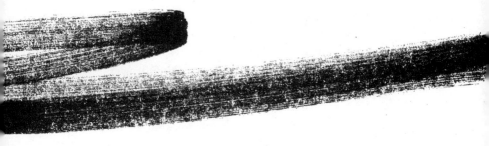

Transition: Not the Worst, the Least Violence

We now enter into some of Derrida's most difficult and yet most powerful argumentation: his criticism of the phenomenological "as such," without which, according to Heidegger, there is no understanding, not even the understanding of death. Before I turn to this argumentation, I'd like to summarize what I explored in chapter 1. I tried to set up the possibility of a more sufficient response to what Derrida calls a "war of the species." In Derrida's diagnosis of our today, this war is part of globalization, which is itself a form of war, a form of pacification of all opponents; it is in fact, as Derrida says in "Faith and Knowledge," "globalatinization." But with globalatinization, we see as well that its universal movement erodes the borders between nation-states. The erosion of borders, for Derrida, increases the probability of the worst happening ("more visibly suicidal than ever"). In chapter 1, I looked at the structure of the worst; in short, it amounts to making two into one: it is a form of totalization. Or it attempts to separate one from the other in order to make one alone: man apart from animal, man apart from the parasite, man unscathed and apart from the "pharmakon." Because of the structure of the worst, we were led back to Derrida's reading of the *Phaedrus* in "Plato's Pharmacy." There we encountered the pharmakon as the "mixture-element," the element that is itself a mixture. But, more important, we saw the ambivalence of the pharmakon; having no value in itself (it is nevertheless not monovalent), the pharmakon destabilizes all value positing. This destabilization defines "twisting free of Platonism." The pharmakon, then, is violence itself (or even radical evil in the sense of evil at the root, "arche-violence" [DLG 164–165/112]), violence that we are not able (this is an inability) to eliminate, a violence that indicates a fundamental weakness or fault in us, in all living beings. The worst violence, however, consists in precisely the attempt to eliminate the evil of the pharmakon once and for all. In contrast, what we are seeking is a more sufficient response to this worst violence, a response that is more sufficient than the reductionism of biological continuity and the separationism of a metaphysical opposition. All attempts bound up with the question of the self (the *autos* or *ipse*) such as animal rights (based on the idea of human rights) fall into one of these two sides, biological continuism or metaphysical separationism. The more sufficient response means that we do not and should not want to eliminate completely the minimal violence. What we are seeking is a lesser violence, even the least violence. Here, in chapter 2, I will offer a glimpse of this more sufficient response through Derrida's idea of "une analogie décalée," "a staggered analogy." But before I turn to this "staggered analogy" and to the argumentation that I have already mentioned, let me once more examine the idea of totalization (which is the worst violence itself)—or rather the inability to totalize. Let me then turn to the *khōra*.

Introduction: Khōra

In "Plato's Pharmacy," Derrida introduces the *khōra* in the context of a "comparison"—and Derrida italicizes the word "comparison"—a comparison between ideas and letters of the alphabet (DIS 184/159). The word "*stoikeia*," or "elements," is not supposed to be taken in its proper sense when they are applied to ideas, just as the names by which we must call *khōra* must not be taken in their proper sense. Already in "Plato's Pharmacy," Derrida was broaching the problem of the discourse about *khōra*.[1] Yet, starting with "Plato's Pharmacy" and ending with *Rogues*, across "How to Avoid Speaking" and "Faith and Knowledge," Derrida examines the *Timaeus* in order to demonstrate the "anachronism" of *khōra* (K 25/94). How are we to understand this anachronism? In fact, we can say that everything that I am going to speak of here concerns the idea of anachronism.

It is well known that, in the *Timaeus*, Plato recounts a story of the creation of the world. *Khōra* (and Derrida, of course, elides the definite article) is the origin prior to and outside of the world. Being prior to and outside of the world means that *khōra* is the third genus, different from intelligible forms and from sensible things. "She" (*khōra*) is the receptacle, of course, for the imprint of the intelligible forms by means of which "she" generates sensible things. As Derrida stresses however, *khōra* is at once older and younger than all the things she produces (K 75/116). "She" is older than sensible things since they are her "children"; she is younger than they since their forms do not really make an impression on her, leaving her "virginal." This "anachronism"— older and younger at once—means that *khōra* is the receptacle of all things and yet "she" receives without receiving; "she" is the container of all things and yet she is none of the content. Nevertheless, "she" must be called something, "she" must be given a name. The only names we have are the names of things that may be either sensible or intelligible. Being names of things that are either sensible or intelligible, "mother" or "nurse," "gold" or "wax," for example, these names are contained *in khōra*. Therefore, to call *khōra*, one must make use of the contents. Yet, if one must use a name found inside the container to name the container, then the status of that name, as Derrida would say, becomes undecidable. Is the name inside *khōra* or outside "her"? Is the name content or the container? Is the name older than *khōra* or younger than "she"? As you can see, the anachronism results in a paradox of naming.

We can look at this paradox of *khōra* in another way, which in this case is not temporal but spatial. Here we turn from anachronism to the question of limits and *espacement*, "spacing." And just as I said that everything here concerns the idea of anachronism, everything also concerns spacing. In fact, what follows is a kind of definition of spacing. Each time one tries to enclose the container—I'm still speaking of *khōra*—that is the whole, it is necessary to cross the border of the whole and occupy a position outside it. Yet each time one occupies a position outside the whole, the whole is no longer whole since it does not include the position outside. Yet, to be the whole, the whole must be whole and it must include everything. Therefore, one must say that the position occupied is neither interior to the whole nor exterior to the whole, or one must say that it is both interior and exterior, a part of the whole and not a part of the whole. The difference between interior and exterior is no longer certain, no longer determinate. As Derrida says, "[le tout] ne se totalise donc *jamais*" (K 84; my emphasis).[2] And that is why Derrida calls *khōra* "le non-lieu," "the non-place" (K 55/107).

There are three implications of the anachronism and spacing of *khōra*. First, *khōra*'s anachronism and spacing disturb the order of all architectonics. *Khōra*, which is a starting point, is not really a starting point since we cannot determine whether "she" is before or after the things she generates, younger or older than they. We could say that *khōra* is before us and after us; "she" is everywhere around us, which would make us think that "she" is a kind of animal. Yet *khōra* is neither human nor animal nor even divine; that "she" is not divine, as Derrida stresses, distinguishes the apophatic discourse about "her" from the apophatic discourse of Christian negative theology (see CNPP 570/39); it distinguishes "her" from the messianic (FS 27/17, paragraph 21), and I shall return to this distinction in chapter 3. Nevertheless, "she" does not exist in the strict sense of either sensible things or intelligible forms. In fact, "she" is always without form or informal or formless (K 33/97, DIS 186/161, CNPP 583/51). And, as Derrida stresses, the use of "mother," for example, to name *khōra* is not a metaphor, since the traditional concept of metaphor is based on the opposition between sensible and intelligible, the very opposition included in *khōra* but excluded from the formlessness that defines "her." *Khōra* does not even have a sense or an essence or an identity.

The second implication of the anachronism and spacing is that, having the existence neither of sensible things nor of intelligible forms, "she" "exists" only through the name; "she" must be called. But none of the names is, as Derrida says, "le mot juste," the right word (K 25/93). Not being able to be called as such, *khōra*, even though "she" is the third *genos*, does not respond to the question of what is; in fact, insofar as "she" does not respond to this question, "she" again resembles an animal. She always and only appears by means of a comparison, as other and never as such (AAEL 103/54; also PS 289/275), which means, as Derrida says in "Khōra," that "this appeal to the third genus was only the moment of a detour in order to signal toward a genus beyond genus [the term in French here is "genre," which means both genus and gender], beyond categories and above all beyond categorial oppositions, which in the first place allow it to be approached or said" (K 17/90). "She" is nothing but an X (CNPP 570/39).

Let me be clear about this second implication. The first concerned architectonic order. The second makes the question "what is" be no longer pertinent since *khōra* does not exist, since "it" or "she" does not exist as such, since "it" or "she" does not appear, speaking quickly, does not appear phenomenologically. But there is a third implication. The *khōra* is the receptacle for everything; it contains everything; it must. In this regard, as the container for everything, *khōra* is *none* of the content. "She" is necessarily a-human; again we can say that "she" is neither animal nor divine or that "she" is both animal and divine. Yet "she" must also be called, which implies that *khōra* is always captured or imprisoned in one of "her" names, in one of "her" contents, in one of the impressions or imprints. To put this idea in a different way, *khōra* is the third genus for everything, and as that genus "she" includes us. But insofar as we name her "mother," insofar as we anthropomorphize "her," we capture "her," imprison "her." Now, she is gone—she does not respond to *this* name—and nevertheless we, we must carry "her." As I am going to show, everything will depend on the name, on the kind of name, on the singular way in which we name *khōra* or animals. There is one more step in this logic. Bearing "her," we must question precisely who we are. If, following Aristotle,[3] we are defined as *zoon logon eckhon*, as the rational animal, then the question of who we are means that we cannot ignore the question of the animal.

It is well known that all Derrida's reflections on animality engage his reading of Heidegger, especially in his 1985 "*Geschlecht* II: Heidegger's Hand." Indeed, *khōra*, insofar as it is a genus (K 53/106), makes us think of *Geschlecht*, which can be translated into English as "genus" or into French as "genre." But Derrida is explicit about the connection between *khōra* and Heidegger. In the essay "Khōra," Derrida says, "our questions are . . . addressed to certain decisions of Heidegger and to their very horizon, to what forms the horizon of the question of the meaning of being and of its epoch" (K 83/120; also K 46 n. 5/104 n. 5 and DLE 22–23/8, 29/12). For Derrida, these decisions determine Heidegger's interpretations of *khōra*, in *Introduction to Metaphysics* and in *What Is Called Thinking;*[4] the decisions revolve around the idea of gathering, *Versammlung, rassemblement.* As Derrida says in *"Geschlecht* II: Heidegger's Hand," "Gathering together (*Versammlung*) is always what Heidegger privileges" (GS2 438/182).

Thanks to *"Geschlecht* II: Heidegger's Hand," we can see that Heidegger's claim, found in *What Is Called Thinking,* that apes (and more generally animals) have no hand (and have no hand precisely in the singular) implies that they do not have access to gathering, and that means to the phenomenological "as such" (GS4 355/173). And especially they have no access to the "as such" of death.[5] The lack of access to death proper explains why, for Heidegger, animals cannot be the privileged being by means of which one is able to reopen the question of being. They do not question their own being. In contrast, as is well known, *Dasein* is able to question its own being since the possibility of death as such defines its proper being. Only from this possibility is it possible to reopen the question of being. To render uncertain the claim that we, as human existence, as *Dasein,* have access to the "as such" of death therefore will do nothing less than destabilize the entire transcendental architectonic structure of *Being and Time.* As Derrida says on the final page of *L'animal que donc je suis,* "The stakes naturally—I'm not hiding this—are so radical that what is at issue is the 'ontological difference,' the 'question' of being, the whole structure of Heidegger's discourse" (A 219). The whole structure of Heidegger's thought is at stake when we make the separation between human existence and animal life uncertain.

Here I am going to take up, as I have already said, Derrida's very difficult and powerful argumentation against the "as such"; this argumentation, which is found in the second essay of the 1992 *Aporias*, "Awaiting (at) the Arrival," concerns the possibility of a pure or proper autoaffection. But I am going to elaborate on this argumentation by examining three other arguments against pure autoaffection that Derrida has presented, arguments that are just as important and just as powerful: the argument against hearing-oneself-speak found in his 1967 study of Husserl, *La voix et le phénomène* (Voice and phenomenon);[6] then the argument against keeping a secret found in his 1986 essay "Comment ne pas parler"; and finally the argument against sovereignty found in the first essay, "The Reason of the Strongest," of *Rogues* from 2002. This elaboration will allow us to understand the poverty of world that Heidegger attributes to animals in *The Fundamental Problems of Metaphysics* (the course from 1929–1930), which I will understand as suffering.[7] What will become undeniable, as we move forward, is that animals suffer.

The "Confrontation" with Heidegger's Thought

Introduction: The Three Points of the "Confrontation"

At the beginning of any examination of the relationship between Derrida and Heidegger, it seems to me that it is very important to recall the following comment from "Heidegger's Hand": "For I [that is, Derrida] never 'criticize' Heidegger without recalling that this can be done from other places in [Heidegger's] own text. His text could not be homogeneous and is written with two hands, at least" (GS2 447/189). We must never forget, it seems to me, that Derrida's thought is always very close to that of Heidegger. In fact, I think that we have to say that Derrida's thought would not exist without that of Heidegger. Nevertheless, we know that Derrida's thought is also very far away from that of Heidegger. Let me accentuate this distance as Derrida himself has done in "Acts: The Meaning of a Given Word," at the end of *Memoires for Paul de Man*. There he lays out three "points" of an "Auseinandersetzung" (literally, a "setting over and against one another"), a "confrontation," as we say in English, between his own thought and, as he says, "a certain voice of Heidegger" (a phrase that makes us recall the heterogeneity of Heidegger's text) (MDM 134/139). The three points are as follows: First, for Heidegger, the essence of technology and by extension rhetoric— Derrida has been speaking of de Man's understanding of rhetoric—is nothing technological or rhetorical. In contrast, for "deconstruction," that is, Derrida's thought, the essence of technology and the thinking of this essence retain something technological; similarly, the thinking of rhetoric is not foreign to rhetoric. Not being foreign to one another, the opposition between technology, which is the accident, and the essence of technology becomes impossible. In deconstruction, there is always "parasitical contamination," and contamination always disturbs architectonic order. The second point also concerns architectonic order: Derrida claims that "memory without anteriority" cannot become a Heideggerian theme. Heidegger's text maintains an indispensable reference to originarity. This point means that, in Heidegger, memory is always a modification or repetition of an origin, of a past that was present. In Derrida, however, memory is first, which means that repetition (and therefore writing and therefore technology) is first: the memory not of a past present but the memory of a past that was never present. Any originarism, outside of and sheltered from technology and writing, is therefore to be deconstructed (MDM 136/141). And then, most important, we have the third point. According to Derrida, for Heidegger, the essence of memory resides in gathering (see also

GS2 439/182). Gathering, in Heidegger, determines the *logos* and language through the idea of *legein*. The *logos* gathers into an "as such," into essence, into the unconcealment of truth in presence and nakedness, into simplicity and propriety. In contrast, in deconstruction, in Derrida's thought, there is no gathering that does not have a "nodal resistance" (DLE 24/9; cf. FS 84/64); gathering never reduces the "disjunctive difference" (MDM 136/141); there is always dispersion, complexity, and impropriety. There is always violence. A different kind of *logos*, which we have seen already through the "pharmakon" and through the naming of *khōra*, prohibits violently the gathering of the disjunction. To put this as simply as possible, it prohibits the gathering of the disjunction into presence, which means that something presents itself without any mediation right before my eyes right now, in the moment.

Animals Have No Hand
(The Privation of the "As Such" of Beings)

It is this idea of gathering that supports Heidegger's claim, in *What Is Called Thinking*, that animals "have [there is not even a "perhaps," *"vielleicht,"* or *"peut-être"* here] no hand" (see GS2 428/173). The context for this claim is, as the title of the book indicates, thought. Heidegger calls thinking *Handwerk*, a work of the hand.[8] But handiwork is not grasping, and here Heidegger plays on the literal meaning of the word "concept" (*Begriff*), which implies grasping or taking. Thinking for Heidegger is not conceptual; the hand is not for grasping. Apes therefore do not think because they have no hand (*er hat keine Hand*); they have only prehensile organs. Heidegger says, "the hand is infinitely different from all grasping organs—paws, claws, or fangs—different by an *abyss* of essence."[9] This abyss of essence places a gap or separation between the hand and the prehensile organs, between "the human *Geschlecht*, our *Geschlecht*, and the animal *Geschlecht*" (GS2 428/173).[10] The hand is a thing apart from the prehensile organ.

Now, according to Derrida in "*Geschlecht* II: Heidegger's Hand," the separation between prehensile organs and the hand really concerns the difference between giving and taking (GS2 430/174–75). Derrida stresses that, in *What Is Called Thinking*—and Derrida quotes this passage at length—Heidegger's hand is not just for giving something but for giving *itself* (*sie recht sich, s'offre*). In this reflexive verb, we see the problem of autoaffection: the hand gives purely when it gives itself, when it gives the same, *autos*. This nontransitive gift, this gift of itself—in English, of course, we can say "give me a hand"—is what really defines the hand for Heidegger. For Heidegger, as Derrida stresses, "the prehensile organ can *only* [Derrida's emphasis] take hold of [*prendre*] and manipulate the thing insofar as, in any case, it does not have to deal with the thing as such, does not let the thing be what it is in its essence. The organ has no access to the essence of the being as such" (GS2 431–32/175; Derrida's emphasis; see also A 63/ATIA 407, DLE 83–84/53, and GS4 377–378/187).[11] Let me anticipate a bit here. Derrida's question is: is it possible to make a separation between giving and taking? In order to give itself, the hand, it seems to me, must take the place of something else. For example, if I give my life for you, I take my life from myself. If I give my hand to your hand, I take the place of the space open in your palm for your other hand or for any other hand. If it is not possible to separate giving and taking, then in the background here in "*Geschlecht* II: Heidegger's Hand" we see Derrida's old problem with the difference between indication and expression, in particular with the general sense of "pointing," "*montrer*," or "*zeigen*" (see VP 24/23, 63/56, and 80/72). This old problem concerns the indeterminate sense of showing, a sense that is prior to the distinction between indication and expression. If man is a sign, as

Heidegger quotes Hölderlin's "Mnemosyne" in *What Is Called Thinking*, then doesn't he rely on the structure of replacement (VP 98–99/88–89) that precedes giving and taking, on the indeterminate structure of pointing, a structure on which the sign making of animals also relies? Is it possible to separate the pointing with the finger of man from the sign making of animals when they trace paths with their paws? So we can see that what Heidegger calls an abyss of essence depends on the question of language. The animal for Heidegger cannot name (and as we see in "The Animal that Therefore I Am [More to Follow]," it is always named [A 54/400]). Yet, to quote Derrida once more, this time from *Of Spirit*, "this inability to name is not primarily or simply linguistic; it derives from the properly *phenomenological* impossibility of speaking the phenomenon whose phenomenality as such, or whose very *as such*, does not appear to the animal and does not unveil the being of the being [*étant*]" (DLE 84/53; Derrida's emphasis; see also DQD 112/67). For Heidegger, animalistic signs, quite simply, do not grant access to the "as such." In other words, animals cannot do phenomenology (although—this is also a strange consequence—Heidegger's "abyss of essence" implies that animals think conceptually, maybe like machines). In any case, and this is the central point, animals do not have access to the "as such" or to gathering. Animals therefore are deprived of the hand, which means that they are deprived of language. What is the nature of this privation?

Derrida's crucial discussion of privation occurs not in "*Geschlecht* II" but in *Of Spirit*, a chronological study of Heidegger's use of the word "*Geist*," starting with *Being and Time* and ending with Heidegger's discussion of Trakl's poetry in the 1950's.[12] For obvious reasons (Heidegger's political involvements), Derrida pauses at Heidegger's writings from the 1930s, in particular at *Introduction to Metaphysics*. In that work, Derrida reminds us (DLE 75/47), Heidegger says, on the one hand, that the world is always a spiritual world, *geistig*, and, on the other, that the animal has neither world nor environment (*Umwelt*, in German). According to Derrida, these comments mean that "animality is not of spirit" (not being "of spirit" also implies that they are not evil or finite), since, as we can see, being "*geistig*" defines a world, of which they have none (DLE 76/47). But, as Derrida immediately points out, these comments from *Introduction to Metaphysics* seem to contradict the three "theses" about world that Heidegger presented three years earlier in *Fundamental Concepts of Metaphysics* (cf. PS 291/277). These three theses are well known. Here they are: (1) The stone is without world (*weltlos*); (2) The animal is poor in world (*weltarm*); and (3) Man is world-forming (*weltbildend*). The question for Derrida is: what does world-poor mean? This is still the question of privation.[13]

The word "poverty" (*Armut, pauvreté*) (to which I shall return in a moment) found in the second thesis could enclose, Derrida claims, two hypotheses (DLE 77/48; see also A 113). First, poverty could imply a difference of degree separating indigence from wealth, in which case man would be rich in world and in spirit, and the animal poor. Second, if the animal is poor in world, the animal must have *some* world—a little, not a lot—and thus some spirit; after all, Heidegger distinguishes the animal from the stone, which is indeed worldless and a-spiritual. Heidegger, however, rejects the first "difference of degree" hypothesis. If the animal has a world, its world is not a species or a degree of the human world. The difference is one not of degree but of essence. The animal lacks world, it does not have enough world, but this is not a quantitative relation to the entities of the world; it is not the case that the animal has less access to things than human existence has: "[the animal] has an *other* relation to beings" (DLE 78/49; Derrida's emphasis). In this discussion, we are very close to Derrida's own thinking. As he shows quite clearly, Heidegger's logic seems to want to combine a lack, a "privation" (*Entbehrung*), which implies degrees, with a difference of alterity. "The lack of the world for the animal," Derrida says, "is not a pure nothingness, but it must *not* be referred, on a scale of homogeneous degree, to a plentitude, *or* to a non-lack [*weltlos*: no world] in a heterogeneous order, for example that of man" (DLE 78/49; my emphasis). Derrida is saying that, for Heidegger, animals in their world poverty have something of the world; their lack is not a "pure nothingness"; they are not "*weltlos*." But, insofar as they have some world, insofar as they have something positive, their world must not be measured, on a homogeneous quantitative scale, by the plentitude of the human world. In order to remove the animal world from a quantitative scale determined by the human world, however, one must not assert that they have nothing at all like a world, nothing at all like a human world; if one did that, one would turn the animal's poverty into a mere negation, which would turn the animals into stones. So, as Derrida concludes, the poverty of the animal has to be absolutely different from that of the stone—the animals have some world—they are not *weltlos*—and yet the poverty of the animals must be absolutely different from the having world of man, since the animals' world is not a mere difference of degree from the human world. This is a difficult idea.

The difficulties of the logic, for Derrida, seem to evolve out of the fact that Heidegger claims that animals can have world, that they have a power, but a power not actualized. But, if their poverty comes from an unactualized possibility, then isn't it possible to say that man, too, may be deprived of world? He has possibilities that are not actualized (DLE 79/49–50). He may not form a world; world may remain hidden in him—here we could introduce the Greek term "*steresis*" again[14]—just as it is hidden in the animals. We are in the vicinity of the risks of which I spoke in chapter 1: biological continuism and metaphysical separationism. Heidegger's analysis respects a difference of structure and looks to break with a difference of degree, with continuism. But it seems not to avoid anthropocentrism because of the idea of privation. Lack or privation, according to Derrida, can take on meaning only from a nonanimal world; or a negation separates animal world poverty from the human world. Now, the idea of nonanimal world refers us back to the questioning "we" of *Dasein*. In order to be world forming, in order to have an understanding of the world (*Weltverstehen*), we must have access to the "as such" of beings. And to have access to the "as such" of beings, we must question our own being. We cannot be indifferent to our own being (cf. DLE 79/49–50). Animals, however, for Heidegger, even with their prehensile organs, never point at themselves (even though we seem to have a fragile distinction between giving and taking). They never, for Heidegger, say "*ego sum.*" And the reason for this lack lies in the fact that animals do not properly die: animals only perish (*verenden*) (cf. AP 76/39, 84/44). Human existence, however, *Dasein*, we have access, according to Heidegger, to death as such: we die (*sterben*). For this reason, we are the privileged "we" with which *Being and Time* opens. The privileged "we" sets up the transcendental architectonic that organizes all of *Being and Time*, making all other empirical investigations of death derivative. I have already quoted this comment from Derrida, but it bears repeating: "The stakes naturally—I'm not hiding this—are so radical that what is at issue is the 'ontological difference,' the 'question' of being, the whole structure of Heidegger's discourse" (A 219).

Dasein Stands Before Itself
(The Privation of the "As Such" of Death)

It seems to me that the argumentation that Derrida uses to destabilize "the whole structure" occurs in *Aporias*, especially in the second essay, "Awaiting (at) the Arrival" ("S'attendre à l'arrivée").[15]

His target is, indeed, the transcendental architectonic of *Being and Time*. In "Awaiting (at) the Arrival," Derrida says, "[Heidegger's] order of order [that is, the method Heidegger follows in *Being and Time*] belongs to the great ontological-juridico-transcendental tradition, and I believe it is undeniable, impossible to dismantle [*indémontable*], and invulnerable (at least this is the hypothesis that I am following here)—except [*sauf*] perhaps in this particular case called death." The uniqueness of the case of death, as Derrida goes on to show, "excludes it from the system of *possibilities* and specifically from the order that it may, in turn, condition" (AP 86–87/45; my emphasis). The word "possibility" in this quotation is very important. As I have already stressed, the result of the dismantling will not be that now we have to say that animals have access to death as such. Rather, what Derrida is trying to show is that humans, as *Dasein*, like animals, do not have that access either.

The weight of Heidegger's structure for Derrida bears upon the ontological difference between *Dasein's* being and *Vorhandenheit* and *Zuhandenheit* (present-at-hand and ready-to-hand, as we say in English). Derrida points out that, in paragraph 49 of *Being and Time*, Heidegger claims that all the anthropological or biological ways of interpreting death forget the essence of *Dasein*. The essence of *Dasein* as a being, its proper being, is precisely possibility, the being-possible: *Möglichkeit*. The idea of possibility—and the composition of this idea is crucial for Derrida—"brings together *on the one hand* [my emphasis] the sense of the virtuality or of the imminence of the future, of the 'that can always happen [*arriver*] at any instant,' it *is necessary to expect it, I am expecting it, we are expecting it* [*il faut s'y attendre, je m'y attends, nous nous y attendons*; Derrida's emphasis] and *on the other hand* [my emphasis] the sense of ability, of the possible as that of which I am capable, that for which I have the power [*puissance*], the ability [*pouvoir*] or the potentiality" (AP 113/62). In short,

"*Möglichkeit*" has two senses: imminence and ability.[16] On the basis of these two senses of possibility, Derrida extracts from *Being and Time* "two typical ontological statements" concerning possibility, but these two statements are inseparable, forming "a single," as Derrida says, "aporetic sentence" (AP 115/64).

Here is the first ontological statement. Death is not just a possibility for *Dasein*; it is *Dasein*'s most proper possibility; in other words, the possibility of death defines what most belongs to *Dasein*, what *Dasein* most owns. Derrida stresses the following passage from paragraph 50: "Death is a possibility-of-being that *Dasein* itself has *to take over* in every case [*zu übernehmen*: with the verb "*nehmen*," "take," we are not very far from the problem of the hand; but let us continue with the quotation]. With death, *Dasein stands before itself* [*steht sich . . . bevor*] in its own potentiality for being (p. 250)" (AP 115–16/64; my emphasis)[17] This quotation makes use of the Macquarrie-Robinson English translation of *Being and Time* that renders "steht sich bevor" as "stands before itself."[18] Derrida, however, renders "steht sich bevor" by means of the French verb "*s'attendre*." There are three ways of interpreting the French reflexive verb "*s'attendre*," according to Derrida. First, there can be a reflexive construction with no object, in which case I await myself: one simply awaits oneself (*on s'attend soi-même*). This interpretation is tautological; *Dasein* awaits itself as waiting for the possibility that is most its own, the same as itself. But then, second, we can add an object to the sentence, which requires a preposition, the "*à*," or the "to." Then we have transitivity, which relates the waiting to something else, to the other, which brings us to what might happen, to what Derrida here calls the "*arrivant*" (AP 117/65). This interpretation is heterological. *Dasein* awaits itself, but this "itself" is, in the second interpretation, other than itself. This composition of same and other brings us to the third interpretation, which associates the tautological with the heterological. The verb "*s'attendre*" can be interpreted as both transitive and reflexive: "wait for each other," "s'attendre l'un l'autre." This construction amounts to a kind of double transitivity (*to* oneself and *to* the other). But the construction is even more heterological when the waiting for each other is related to death (AP 117/65). Even though death is what most defines *Dasein*'s propriety, it is always other since this "what can always happen or arrive" takes what is most one's own away. It takes all possibilities away.

But in order to understand really the heterological nature of the construction, we must return to Heidegger's German preposition "*bevor*." As in English—and here Derrida explicitly quotes the Macquarrie-Robinson English translation of *Being and Time* (AP 119/66)—this preposition can have a temporal sense and a spatial sense. In fact, Derrida splits the two senses into two French prepositions, "*avant*" (which is temporal) and "*devant*" (which is spatial). If in death I am "standing before myself," then "before" is "*devant*," which implies some distance from myself, myself as another, as in "standing before a mirror" (AP 119/66). The other then is over there; death is over there; there is, as Derrida would say, "espacement." I have, of course, spoken of *espacement* in relation to the *pharmakon* and *khōra*. Passing now to the temporal sense of the preposition, we can say that, in death, I stand "before" myself, "*avant*," earlier, which means that I, me myself, am already out there at the limit of death. If I am already out there, over there and not here, then I have already, earlier, died. If I have already died, then my waiting for myself is late or, more precisely, later; I've missed my rendezvous. The simplest way to understand this lateness is to recognize that, if what most properly defines me is the possibility of death, then what I am most fundamentally is a process of dying. From the very first moment, as soon as I have taken the very first breath or the very first heartbeat, I have the possibility of dying, of suffocating or having a heart attack, which means that, in a sense, I have already died, which means that my death is always already in the past. My death is what I find myself with from the very first moment. Or we can think about the lateness in the following way. The lateness is an essential necessity when what I am waiting for is my death: if I made the rendezvous, then I would be dead, and I would therefore no longer be there and would miss the rendezvous; or, if I am still alive and still here, then I am not there, not dead, and once again the rendezvous has been missed. In short, *Dasein's* standing before itself in death makes the simultaneity of the one and the other impossible. As Derrida says, "Death is ultimately the name of the impossible simultaneity and of an impossibility that we know simultaneously, at which we await for each other however together, at the same time, *ama* as one says in Greek: at the same time, simultaneously, we wait for each other at this anachrony and at this *contretemps*" (AP 117–118/65). We also saw this anachronism with *khōra*. But "*contretemps*" is a word Derrida borrows from Levinas. So we could quote Levinas, from *Otherwise than Being*: "In approaching the other, I am always late for the rendezvous."[19] Or we could quote Blanchot, from *The Writing of the Disaster*: "the imminence of what has already happened" (D 60/49). As Derrida says in *Demeure*, "this is an *unbelievable* tense [*voilà un temps incroyable*]" (D 60/49; Derrida's emphasis). But this comment anticipates too much. The first ontological statement concerns lateness or anachrony (which means nonsimultaneity). The second concerns the "as such" of death.

So, let us now pass to the second ontological statement concerning possibility that Derrida extracts from *Being and Time*. In paragraph 50, Heidegger ultimately says that death is for *Dasein* the possibility of an impossibility. As Derrida says, this "nuclear proposition" is frequently cited, but the question is where do we situate it: in the possibility of an impossibility or the impossibility of a possibility (AP 121/68)? Heidegger first describes the impossibility as "the possibility of no longer being able to be there" (*Sein und Zeit*, paragraph 50, p. 250). This is, indeed, the possibility of no longer being able, but not the impossibility of a being able to. We are again very close to Derrida's own thinking. Derrida says, "The nuance is thin, but its very fragility is what seems to me both decisive and significant, and it is probably most essential in Heidegger's view. Death, the most proper possibility of *Dasein*, is the possibility of a being-able-no-longer-to-be-there or of a no longer being able to be there as *Dasein*" (AP 122/68). Heidegger, for Derrida, seems to be speaking of an ability to be unable or an inability to be able.

We come now to an important transition in the analysis. In paragraph 52, however, Heidegger opens the question of truth because of the everyday certainty of death. The association we need to make here is to truth as certainty. Now, according to Derrida, Heidegger seems to see in the contradiction between possibility and impossibility the condition of truth, its very unveiling, where truth is no longer measured in terms of the logical form of the judgment (AP 124/70), where it is no longer measured by certainty, where truth is originary truth, *aletheia*. The question of truth as unconcealment (*aletheia*) takes us into the question of the "as such." Derrida turns to paragraph 53, where Heidegger says: "The nearest nearness of being-towards-death as possibility is as far removed as possible from anything real [*Wirklichen*]. The more clearly this possibility is understood, the more purely does understanding penetrate it *as* [*als*] the possibility of the impossibility of existence [*Existenz*] in general" (*Sein und Zeit*, p. 262; my emphasis of the "as," not Derrida's). Derrida comments on each of these two sentences in turn. The first sentence, as we just saw, concerns the relation between death and actuality or reality (*Wirklichkeit*). It means that death is what is closest to us; we have the absolute proximity of death. But death is also as far away as possible and as far away as possible from any actual reality; therefore death is not a possibility that modifies an actual reality; it is not the possibility *of something*. If it does not give us something to actualize, then death must be thought of as the possibility of something that is not real, of something that is impossible, as the possibility of an impossible. The possibility of death therefore exceeds the standard relation of potentiality and actuality. But then Derrida turns to the second sentence, which concerns understanding; he says, "in the [second] sentence, the figure of unveiling, that is, the truth of this syntax, makes the impossible be, in the genitive form, the complement of the noun or the aporetic supplement of the possible (possibility of the impossible), *but also* [my emphasis] the manifestation of the possible *as* impossible, the 'as' (the 'als') becoming the enigmatic figure of this monstrous coupling" (AP 124/70). The "*als*" in the second sentence means that the possibility is understood, that is, both unveiled and penetrated as impossibility. It is possibility as impossibility, the proper possibility of *Dasein* as its proper impossibility.[20] For Derrida, and this is crucial: if possibility is what most properly defines *Dasein*'s being—*Dasein* is not *Vorhandenheit* or *Zuhandenheit*, and neither is *Dasein* an animal—then *Dasein*'s proper possibility as im-possibility, proper possibility as the negation of *Dasein*'s proper possibility, this "as" makes death be *Dasein*'s "least proper" possibility (AP 125/71). This is an important quotation: Derrida says, "the *als* (*as*, considered as) keeps in reserve the most unthinkable but it is not yet the *als solche* (as such): we will have to ask ourselves how a most proper possibility as impossibility can still speak as such without immediately disappearing, without the 'as such' already sinking beforehand and without its essential disappearance making *Dasein* lose everything that distinguished it—both from other forms of entities and even from the living animal in general, from the beast. And without its properly dying being, originally contaminated and parasited by the perishing and the demising" (AP 125–

126/71). The question we must ask now is obvious: if *Dasein* does not have access to the "as such" of death, if *Dasein* has access to its most proper possibility only as mediated by the "as" of impossibility, then is *Dasein*'s hand separated by "an abyss of essence" from the ape's prehensile organ?

The Elaboration of the Argumentation Against the "As Such"

Let me say again that the argumentation we have just gone through, from "Awaiting (at) the Arrival" in *Aporias* (from 1992), ranks among the most important that Derrida ever produced. Minimally, we can say that, insofar as the argumentation focuses on *Dasein* standing before itself, it concerns the mirror, "une psyché," as Derrida would say: "a mirror is sufficient [*un miroir peut y suffire*]" (ASAR 167/124). One could say that fundamentally what Derrida is trying to do in his writings on animality is to move back Lacan's mirror stage, which in Lacan divided human from animals; Derrida is trying to place this division or even the symbolic into animal life itself. Overall, the mirror stage concerns autoaffection. In *L'animal que donc je suis*, Derrida tells us what he is trying to do with autoaffection: "if the auto-position, the auto-monstration of the auto-directedness of the I, even in man, implied the I as an other and had to welcome in the self some irreducible hetero-affection (which I [that is, Derrida] have attempted elsewhere), then this autonomy of the I would be neither pure nor rigorous; it would not be able to give way to a simple and linear delimitation between man and animal" (A 133). Of course, no one would deny autoaffection of animals. In other words, what is at issue is animal narcissism (A 77/ATIA 418). It is not hard to find arguments that would lead toward the assertion of animal narcissism. For instance, one member of a species always recognizes another of the same species, and thus we can say that there is some self-recognition (A 88). There is also the fact that animals become sexually aroused at the sight of a partner, which means the animals have some sense of erotic exposure and thus nudity (A 89). And there is also the common experience that all of us have had with our house pets: the cat stops for a moment to watch television when there are cats in the program on the screen. If we can respond in the affirmative to the question of animal narcissism, then we have to say that the animal is caught in the same mirror as I, even that the animal is in me, as the other in me (A 77/ATIA 418; ASAR 181/134). But, in order to elaborate on the powerful argumentation of *Aporias*, let us look at three of these "other places" where Derrida has spoken of an irreducible heteroaffection in autoaffection.

The first occurs, as I said at the beginning, in *La voix et le phé-nomène* (*Voice and Phenomenon*), Derrida's 1967 study of Husserl. Here Derrida argues that, when Husserl describes lived experience (*Erlebnis*), even absolute subjectivity, he is speaking of an interior monologue, autoaffection as hearing-oneself-speak. According to Derrida, hearing-oneself-speak is, for *Husserl*, "an absolutely unique kind of auto-affection" (VP 88/78). It is unique because there seems to be no external detour from the hearing to the speaking; in hearing-oneself-speak there is self-proximity. It seems therefore that I hear myself speak immediately, in the very moment that I am speaking. According to Derrida, Husserl's own description of temporalization undermines the idea that I hear myself speak immediately. On the one hand, Husserl describes what he calls the "living present," the present that I am experiencing right now, as being perception, and yet he also says that the living present is thick. The living present is thick because it includes phases other than the now, in particular, what Husserl calls "protention," the anticipation (or "awaiting," we might say) of the approaching future and "retention," the memory of the recent past. As is well known, Derrida focuses on the status of retention in *Voice and Phenomenon*. Retention in Husserl has a strange status since he wants to include it in the present as a kind of perception and at the same time he recognizes that it is different from the present as a kind of nonperception. For Derrida, Husserl's descriptions imply that the living present, by always folding the recent past back into itself, by always folding memory into perception, involves a difference in the very middle of it (VP 77/69).[21] In other words, in the very moment when silently I speak to myself, it must be the case that there is a minuscule hiatus differentiating me into the speaker and into the hearer. There must be a hiatus (*un écart*) that differentiates me from myself, a hiatus or gap without which I would not be a hearer as well as a speaker. This hiatus defines what Derrida has always called the trace, a minimal repeatability. And this hiatus, this fold of repetition, is found in the very moment of hearing-myself-speak. Derrida stresses that "moment" or "instant" translates the German "*Augenblick*," which literally means "blink of the eye." When Derrida stresses the literal meaning of "*Augenblick*," he is in effect deconstructing auditory autoaffection into visual autoaffection. When I look in the mirror, for example, it is necessary that ("il faut que," Derrida would say) I am "distanced" or "spaced" from the mirror. I must be distanced from myself so that I am able to be both seer and seen. The space between, however, remains (as Foucault would say) "obstinately invisible."[22] Remaining invisible, the space gouges out the eye, blinds it. I see myself over there in the mirror, and yet that self over there is other than I, so I am not able to see myself as such. What Derrida is trying to demonstrate here is that this "spacing" (*espacement* again)[23] or blindness is essentially necessary for all forms of autoaffection, even tactile autoaffection, which seems to be immediate. Here again, we could open the question of the hands. For Derrida, and here he is perhaps quite distant from

Merleau-Ponty, the touching-touched relation is a variant of the seeing-seen relation because in vision there is always spacing. When one hand touches the other, even in prayer, the coincidence of the touching-touched is only ever imminent, fusion only ever about to happen or arrive. It is as if in the gathering of the fingers, there is a gouged-out eye that forbids the gathering of being into any "as such."[24]

Now, let us go to another "other place," which can be found in "Comment ne pas parler." Here Derrida discusses negative theology by means of the idea of "dénégation," "denegation" or "denial." The word "*dénégation*" translates Freud's "*Verneinung*," which is in fact a denial, but one that is also an affirmation. The fundamental question, then, for negative theology but also psychoanalysis and for Derrida, is how to deny and yet also not deny. This duality between not telling and telling is why Derrida takes up the idea of the secret. In "Comment ne pas parler," Derrida says, and this is an important comment for understanding the secret in Derrida: "There is a secret of denial [*dénégation*] and a denial [*dénégation*] of the secret. The secret *as such*, as secret, separates and already institutes a negativity; it is a negation that denies itself. It de-negates itself" (CNPP 557/25; my emphasis). Here Derrida speaks of a secret as such. A secret as such is something that must not be spoken; we then have the first negation: "I promise not to give the secret away." And yet, in order to possess a secret really, to have it really, I must tell it to myself. Here we can see the relation of hearing-oneself-speak that we just saw in *Voice and Phenomenon*. Keeping a secret includes necessarily autoaffection. We might, however, say more; we might even say that I am too weak for this not to happen. I must have a conceptual grasp of it; even more, we might say that I have to frame a representation of the secret. With the idea of a representation, we also see retention, repetition, and the trace or a name. A trace of the secret must be formed, in which case, the secret is in principle shareable. If the secret must be necessarily shareable, it is always already shared. In other words, in order to frame the representation of the secret, I must negate the first negation, in which I promise not to tell the secret; I thereby make a second negation, a "denegation," which means I must break the promise not to tell the secret. In order to keep (*garder*) the secret (or the promise), I must necessarily not keep the secret (I must violate the promise). So, I possess the secret and do not possess it. This structure—once again we could speak of a kind of anachronism or *espacement* in autoaffection—has the consequence of there being no secret as such: a secret is necessarily shared (*partagé*). As Derrida says in "Comment ne pas parler," "This denial [*dénégation*] does not happen [to the secret] by accident; it is essential and originary. . . . The enigma . . . is the sharing [*le partage*] of the secret, and not only shared to my partner in the society but the secret shared within itself, its 'own' partition, which divides the essence of a secret that cannot even appear to one alone except in starting to be lost, to divulge itself, hence to dissimulate itself, as secret, in showing itself: dissimulating its dissimulation. There is no secret as such; I deny it. And this is what I confide in secret to whomever allies himself to me. This is the secret of the alliance" (CNPP 557/25). This quotation presents the condition for joining what I would call "the alliance of a more sufficient response": the denial of the "as such." As I shall show in chapter 3, we must let the animals slip away from any "as such." We are able to be this weak.

Now, finally, let us go to one of the most recent of Derrida's writings, to his 2002 "The Reason of the Strongest," the first essay in the book called *Rogues*. There Derrida is discussing the United Nations, which he says combines the two principles of Western political thought: sovereignty and democracy.[25] But "democracy and sovereignty are at the same time, but also by turns, inseparable and in contradiction with one another" (V

143/100). Democracy and sovereignty are inseparable because, in order for democracy to be effective, it must have a sovereign force. And yet sovereignty contradicts democracy because sovereignty, pure sovereignty, the very "essence of sovereignty" (V 143/100), is silent, it does not have to give reasons, it "always keeps quiet in the very ipseity of the moment proper to it, a moment that is but the stigmatic point of an indivisible instant. A pure sovereignty is indivisible or it is not at all" (V 143/100–101). In other words, sovereignty attempts to possess power indivisibly, it tries not to share, and not sharing means contracting power into an instant—the instant of action, of an event, of a singularity. We can see the outline here of Derrida's deconstruction not only of the hearing-oneself-speak autoaffection but also of the autoaffection of the promising-to-oneself-to-keep-a-secret. When power is contracted into an instant, there is no temporal thickness; the instant is withdrawn from temporalization and even from history. But such a withdrawal explains why sovereignty is always silent; it tries to keep its power secret. If power is to be sovereign and indivisible, it cannot participate in language, which introduces universalization and sharing (*partager*). Sovereignty is incompatible with universalization, with the minimal repetition of the trace, which divides the instant and opens up the distance of the hiatus. And yet the concept of democracy calls for universalization, even though there can be no democracy without force, without freedom, without a decision, without sovereignty. In democracy, a decision is always urgent, and yet (here is the contradiction) democracy takes time, democracy makes one wait. Power can never be exercised without its communication; as Derrida says, "as soon as I speak to the other, I submit to the law of giving reason(s), I share a virtually universalizable medium, I divide my authority" (V 144/101). As soon as there is sovereignty, there is abuse of power; sovereignty can reign only by not sharing. There must be sovereignty, and yet there can be no use of power without the sharing of it through repetition. More precisely, as Derrida says, "since [sovereignty] never succeeds in [not sharing] except in a critical, precarious, and unstable fashion, sovereignty can only *tend* [*tendre*; Derrida's emphasis], for a limited time, to reign without sharing. It can only tend toward imperial hegemony. To make use of the time is already an abuse—and this is true as well for *the rogue that I therefore am* [*le voyou que donc je suis*: the rogue that therefore I follow]" (V 146/102; my emphasis). This tendency defines the worst, a tendency toward the complete appropriation of all others, including animals. I do not need to stress, of course, that with the idea of rogues, especially through the English word, we have not left behind the question of animals. Sovereign power is never given as such, even to the sovereign, who is frequently described as an animal: the leviathan.[26]

Conclusion: The Undeniability of Animal Suffering

We have now seen four variants of the same argument against the "as such" or against presence, one in "Awaiting (at) the Arrival," one in *Voice and Phenomenon*, one in "Comment ne pas parler," and, finally, one in "The Reason of the Strongest." What these arguments attack is an axiom that, Derrida says, is an "unvarying truth" in every discourse concerning the animal, especially those found "in the Western philosophical discourse" (A 70/ATIA 413). This axiom allows man to grant precisely to himself that of which the animal would be deprived (A 133). Let us consider the animal privation one more time, and this time I am going to add in more implications. According to Heidegger, the ape, animals in general, are deprived of the hand. This first, "manual" privation of the animal implies that animals do not possess the ability to speak or, more precisely, to make apophantic language; they cannot say "S is P" because they do not have access to the "as such" of beings (cf. VP 81/72–73). In a word, animals are deprived of gathering. Now here is an implication we have not yet seen. Being deprived of the "as such" or the essence of things, the animal is not able to lie (ASAR 175/130). Not being phenomenologists, animals are not given things in their unconcealment, in their truth, which would grant them the possibility of trying to hide the truth, to keep the truth secret. This privation of the lie implies, of course, that animals do not know good from evil (ASAR 178/132). The lack of knowledge seems then to imply a kind of perfection or plentitude to the animal (ASAR 167/124). With the "then," we have just crossed a strange transition in which a lack leads to a plentitude. Because of a fault, man conceives animals as being absolutely innocent, prior to good and evil, "without fault or defect" (*sans faute et sans défaut*) (A 133). The animals therefore do not seem to suffer a fall. But the perfection that animals possess is that of a machine, the "animal-machine" (ASAR 172/127).[27] Like writing, animals only ever react (cf. DIS 165/143); they do not ask questions, and they do not respond (DLE 82/52; A 24–25/377–78, 168/124). In contrast, man is not perfect; he has fallen and has a fault, which allows him to question. The ability to question brings us to the axiom: it is precisely "a fault or defect [*une faute* or *un défaut*]" in man, in us, that allows us to be masters over the animals; in other words, the superiority of animals makes them inferior to us (A 40/ATIA 389). Derrida says, "what is proper to man, his superiority over and subjugation of the animal, his very becoming-subject, his historicity, his emergence out of nature, his sociality, his access to knowledge and technics, all that, everything (in a non-finite number of predicates) that is proper to man would derive from this originary defect [*défaut*], indeed from this defect in propriety, what is proper to man as defect in propriety" (A 70/ATIA

413). To use the mythological language to which Derrida refers, because man is not a perfect being like the animal, because man is born nude, he receives fire (A 40/ATIA 40/389; A 69/ATIA 412). Or, to use the language of Lacan to which Derrida also refers, it is man's "pre-maturity" that separates him from the animals and allows man to enter into the symbolic (ASAR 167/124). In a word, with this fault, we are speaking of human finitude (A 49/ATIA 396).[28] It is precisely human finitude that allows man to sacrifice—do we say murder? (cf. PS 297/283)[29]—animals (PS 291/277, 293/279; A 40/389; FL 42–43/18–19; DQD 119/71). Remember that Abraham substitutes a ram for the sacrifice of Isaac. As chapter 3 will discuss, in order to reach a more sufficient response, what must be sacrificed is sacrifice itself.

This axiom about finitude must be questioned. It seems to me that the axiom can be questioned only in the arguments we have seen here. In an essay from 2000 called "Et cetera," Derrida presents the principle that guides the arguments or, as he says, "the demonstrations" that we have just gone through. It in fact defines deconstruction: "Each time that I say 'deconstruction and X (regardless of the concept or the theme),' this is the prelude to a very singular division that turns this X into, or rather makes appear in this X, *an impossibility* that becomes its proper and sole possibility, with the result that between the X as possible and the 'same' X as impossible, there is nothing but a relation of homonymy, a relation for which we have to provide an account. . . . For example, here referring myself to demonstrations I have already attempted . . . , gift, hospitality, death itself (and therefore so many other things) can be possible only *as impossible*, as the impossible, that is, unconditionally."[30]

Let us strip the demonstration down one more time to its essential structure. If what most properly defines human existence is the fault or defect of being mortal, or, more precisely, if understanding the possibility of mortality as possibility is what most properly defines us, then we are able to say that we understand that possibility truly only if we have access to death as such in the presence of a moment, in the blink of the eye, in indivisible and silent sovereignty, secretly. But since we only ever have access to the possibility of death as something other than possibility, that is, as impossibility, as something blinding, as something shared across countless others, we cannot say that we understand the possibility of death truly, naked even. *Then, the being of us, our fault, resembles the fault of animals.*[31] The fault now has been generalized and therefore so has evil. The resemblance between us and them in regard to the fault or evil, however, does not mean that we have anthropomorphized the animals; it does not mean that we have succumbed to the risk of biological continuism. With this resemblance, we have what Derrida, in *Of Spirit*, calls "une analogie décalée," "a staggered analogy" (DLE 81/51; cf. A 113–114). There is a nonsimultaneity between us and them, between us and the other. This nonsimultaneity comes with time or rather is "from time," "depuis le temps," as Derrida says in "The Animal that Therefore I Am (More to Follow)" (A 40/ATIA 390), "from always," "depuis toujours," as he says in "The Ends of Man" (MP 147/123). What these phrases mean is clear: there is a fault, and yet there is no fall. The nonsimultaneity is always there, in all of us, in the *Geschlecht* or genus or genre or gender or race or family or generation that we are; the *Geschlecht* is always *verwesende*, "de-essenced" (DLE 143/91). The fault that divides, being there in us, means that all of us are not quite there, not quite *Da*, not quite dwelling, or, rather, all of us are living out of place, in a sort of nonplace, in the indeterminate place called *khōra*, about which we can say that it is neither animal nor divine—nor human—or that it is both animal and divine—and human. Indeterminate, the nonplace contains countless divisions, countless faults. All of us living together in this nonplace, we see now, is based in the fact that all living beings can end ("Finis," as in the title of the first essay found in *Aporias*) (cf. AP 76/39). All living beings are mortal (A 206), and that means we can speak of "the ends of animal" (A 113). All living beings share in this weakness, in this lack of power, in "this impotence [*impuissance*] at the heart of power" (A 49/ATIA 396). All of us have this fault. Therefore we can return to a question raised earlier: are not all of us "poor in world"? This "poverty," "Ar-mut," in German, implies a "feeling oneself poor," a kind of passion, a kind of suffering (A 213).[32] Therefore, when an animal looks at me, does it not address itself to me, mutely, with its eyes; does it not implore, just as Derrida's cat looks at him, imploring him to set it free (from the bathroom)? And does not this look imply that, like us, animals suffer? The suffering of animals is undeniable (A 49/ATIA 396). And as Derrida always says in relation to these sorts of formulas, this undeniability means that we can only deny it, and deny it in countless ways (CNPP 549/16; FS 77/59). Yet none of these denials of the suffering of animals will have been sufficient!

A More Sufficient Response?

Transition: Sacrifice Must Be Sacrificed

I am seeking a more sufficient response to the violence that man
wages against animals. A more sufficient response is required today because of the condition of globalization, which appears to
be peace but is in fact war by other means. As Derrida says in
Rogues, and I quoted this passage in chapter 1, "a new violence is
being prepared and in truth has been unleashed for some time
now, in a way that is more visibly suicidal . . . than ever" (V
215/156).[1] A more sufficient response, it seems to me, can be determined only by means of avoiding or at least negotiating with
the risks of which I have already spoken: biological continuism
and metaphysical separationism. These two risks amount to the
worst. I have described how the structure of the worst is a question of numbers. As a superlative, the worst is the most violent,
the most suicidal, since in the name of purity it threatens to contaminate everything, since in the name of life it threatens to kill
everything. Every single other is wholly other (*tout autre est tout
autre*), and therefore every single other might be the enemy. The

worst consists in appropriating what is other, making the two identical, or it consists in separating the two, making the one be the negation of the other. In other words, biological continuism makes the two one; metaphysical separationism keeps the two two. But there is another way to express the worst. Metaphysical separationism is Platonism (or Cartesianism); biological continuism, in a word, biologism, is the mere reversal of Platonism. One of my questions has been and continues to be, and I do not think it is an exaggeration to say that this question is the question of our today: is it possible to twist free of Platonism? In either Platonism or the mere reversal of Platonism, there is no elemental mixture, no mixture that precedes the separation into elements. There is only an indivisible limit between the two, between man and animal in this case; the globe—fully enclosed like a circle—the globe of a sovereign subject (*autos*: the same) is constituted. The worst is the worst abuse of power. Although we are not able to make a response that is not violent, that is not evil even in a radical way, we are seeking a response that is the least violent, the least evil, the least powerful, a response that is weak. As Derrida says in *L'animal que donc je suis*, "I was dreaming of inventing an unheard-of grammar . . . in order to make a scene which is neither human nor divine nor animal, a scene aiming at denouncing all the discourses on the so-called animal. . . . As if I were dreaming, in all innocence, of an animal that wanted to do no harm [*mal*] to the animal" (A 93).[2]

I have also demonstrated that this least violent response must result from questioning the axiom that, according to Derrida, has been an unvarying truth in all discourses about animals in the Western tradition. This axiom concerns finitude. It says that precisely because there is a fault or defect in man, man is able to be master over the animals. This axiom allows man to grant to himself that of which the animal would be deprived (A 133). Because man is finite, he has the very ability to speak, he is able to ask questions and to respond, while animals, being somehow perfect, lack the very same ability, to speak, to ask questions, and therefore to respond. In other words, animals, and man insofar as he is the rational animal, do not think. Here we shall confront precisely how to conceive this not-thinking. As I shall show, the privation of animals, their inability or impotence to question, amounts to an indetermination, yet precisely because animal language is indeterminate, animals, even in their silence, do more than question. Their language is connected to their suffering. If we thought like poets (and not like philosophers or scientists), we would wonder why dogs bark in the middle of the night. Do they suffer from bad conscience? Nevertheless, the suffering of animals is so indeterminate that it can be determined in countless ways. Their suffering goes beyond all limits, which means that they suffer like us; their fault is just like our fault—since always. If there is a kind of analogy between our suffering and theirs, then what must happen is that we, we humans, must stop, as much as this is possible, sacrificing animals for our sake. It is necessary that sacrifice itself be sacrificed. Instead of the substitution that defines sacrifice, there must be a kind of saving by means of replacement or even by means of misplacement. In the space that there is (which is neither the world of forms nor the sensible world), we must receive the animals. The more sufficient response to the violence against animals (against all the others) is based only on such a reception. And therefore, to anticipate, we can say that the least violent response is the most amiable response. The more sufficient response is the friendly response.

The path to this amiable response goes through the mirror. Like Foucault, Derrida has always played on the French word "une psyché" (A 76–77/ATIA 418).[3] This French word means "a large wardrobe mirror," but it is also the Greek word for the soul. I quoted before this comment from "And Say the Animal Responded": "a mirror is sufficient [*un miroir peut y suffire*]" (ASAR

167/124). In other words, in the experience of the mirror, we have a specific experience of autoaffection. Since Aristotle, defining the soul by means of the sense of touch, autoaffection has always defined the living. But what Derrida is trying to show with touch is that, despite the apparent immediacy and sameness of touch, there is always a kind of mediation and difference. The mirror is there right between the hands that touch one another, even in the hands that are folded together for prayer. Yet the mirror, with its spacing, with its nonsimultaneity or anachronism, is an experience of blindness; it is even the experience of death. As soon as I see myself, repeated over there in the glass, the one who is seeing is gone. If the seen is there in the mirror, then the seer is, in a sense, dead. Here I could quote the passage from Edgar Allen Poe with which Derrida opens *La voix et le phénomène*: "now—I am dead" (see also CF 94–96/64–66). In the very experience of the now, I have disappeared, I am other than myself and necessarily so, for without being other, I would not see myself as over there in the glass. I can have access to myself as other, but I can never have access to myself, in other words, as such. There is a fault here—the fault is that I am powerless to have access to myself as such—that makes autoaffection always be heteroaffection. But if I am always other in the experience of the mirror, then when I look at myself I really do not know who I am or what I am. Perhaps the me over there in the mirror is really an animal, an animal that therefore I am, an animal that therefore I follow, an animal that therefore I await, an animal that therefore I carry.

Introduction: The Cat's Eyes

Derrida begins "The Animal That Therefore I Am (More to Follow)" by speaking of nudity (A 15/ATIA 369). In nudity, two ideas intersect. On the one hand, nudity refers to truth as un-concealment, which is truth as the "as such." On the other, there is the nudity at the birth of man, the fault, the weakness, the vulnerability that man thinks belongs to him alone. This inter-section is why Derrida can say later in "The Animal that There-fore I Am (More to Follow)" that "the truth of modesty [*pudeur*] will finally be our subject" (A 70/ATIA 413). But the question is: Does this fault, nudity, belong to man alone, as one of his prop-erties? Or is it something we share with all living beings? The shame that goes along with nudity means that we must always cover ourselves up, never appearing as such, always appearing as other than ourselves. Everything comes down to the "as," the "as" that is prior to the "as such" and the "as if" (V 14/xiv), that is prior to the real and the imaginary. We can see here that with nudity we are very close to Lacan's idea of the symbolic.[4]

The problem of nudity arises in the story of the cat that enters Derrida's bathroom in the morning while he is naked. The story is not simple, despite the fact that it describes an experience that is well known, common to anyone who has a cat. The story Der-rida tells starts with a reflexive verb (a reflexive verb always indi-cates autoaffection). In this case, the reflexive verb is "*se de-mander*"; Derrida says, "I often ask myself [*me demande*], just to see, who I am [*qui je suis*] at the moment when, caught naked [*surpris nu*], in silence, by the gaze of an animal, for example the eyes of a cat. I have trouble," as David Wills's English translation goes, using "trouble" to render "*du mal*," "I have trouble, yes, trouble [*du mal*, again] overcoming my embarrassment [*une gêne*]" (A 18/ATIA 372). The autoaffection is hearing-oneself-speak, the very autoaffection that lies at the center of *Voice and Phenomenon*.[5] Derrida is questioning—"*me demande*"—his own being. The self-questioning is provoked by the indifferent, "just to see" gaze of his cat's eyes. The cat that is the other then pro-duces the mirroring relation within Derrida's own self. Being gazed upon by the cat, he asks himself: "who am I?" This autoaffection, in other words, cannot be distinguished from heteroaffection. But there is an emotional reaction to the gaze of the animal, to the gaze of his cat, which is not a figure of a cat but a real cat, the cat who sees him naked. There is a feeling of modesty (*pudeur*) whose "reflex" (*mouvement*) Derrida is at pains "to repress." There is the "impropriety" (*malséance*) "of a certain animal nude before the other animal," and Derrida says that, from that point on, one might call it a kind of *animalséance*:[6] "the single, incomparable and original experience of the impropriety that would come from appearing in truth naked, in front of the insistent gaze of the animal; a benevolent or pitiless gaze, surprised or cognizant. The gaze of a seer, visionary, or extra-lucid blind person" (A 18/ATIA 372). The indifference of this gaze refers us back to what we saw in chapter 1, a gaze, a vision, a seeing that does not posit values, even though the potential for positing is there. The "just to see" of the cat, like any animal, could become interested, valuing what it sees as something to bite and eat, which means the gaze could become threatening. The gaze of the cat could come to resemble therefore the gaze of the man who looks upon the fattened calf. Which is which? The answer to the question of who I am and who you are becomes uncertain. We could say, appropriating a phrase from Deleuze and Guattari, that the experience described in the story of the cat who enters Derrida's bathroom in the morning asking to be fed opens up a "zone of indiscernability."[7]

How are to understand this zone, this undecidability, as Derrida would say? We know that the tradition says that one thing that distinguishes humans from animals is our awareness of our nudity. In contrast, animals seem not to know they are naked; they seem not to be conscious or aware of their nudity, which goes along with their unawareness of good and evil. They seem to feel no shame in their nudity. But, if they feel no shame in their nudity, we could say that they are never really nude since the definition of nudity seems to include awareness of it. Animals then would not be naked because they have no awareness of being naked. But the fact that animals do not experience shame in their nakedness could imply that the animals are in fact clothed at all times. Humans, in contrast, are really naked because they have a sense of modesty. But this sense of modesty (which is the awareness of being naked) means that they can never be naked as animals are, they can never be free of the sense of shame. Therefore having the sense of modesty means that humans, too, are always clothed. Or, in other words and as Derrida says, humans are not naked because they are naked, while animals are naked because they are not naked (A 19/ATIA 373). Or, in still other words, we are, as we say in English, "naked as a jaybird," or we are, as Derrida says in his story, "nu comme une bête," "naked as a beast." But, this "as" remains indiscernible, uncertain, and indeterminate. As Derrida says, "Man could never be naked again [as animals are] because he has the sense of nakedness, that is, of modesty and shame. The animal would be *in* non-nudity because it is nude, and man *in* nudity to the extent that he is no longer nude. There we encounter a difference, a time or a *contretemps* between the two *nudities without nudity*" (A 20/ATIA 374; Derrida's emphasis).

We have seen this lack of simultaneity before. Derrida's story of his cat in fact describes the "staggered analogy" between man and animals of which I spoke in chapter 2. But we see now the difficulty of this idea. The staggered analogy consists in a resemblance between faults. Indeed, the strength of Derrida's story of his cat lies in the distribution of the fault: "something happens there that shouldn't take place—like everything that happens [*arrive*] in the end, a lapsus, a fall, a failure [*défaillance*], a fault [*une faute*]" (A 19/ATIA 373). The fault means that I or you or a cat or any living thing does not have the power to control completely the distribution of the very traits (which are singular) that define me or you or a cat or any living thing. A resemblance between faults therefore brings together or compares two things without a common measurement (CF 73/46). Neither of the two can possess completely a proper characteristic that would determine the other by degrees of difference or by a negation of a quality. The "staggered analogy" is a comparison, we could say, without comparison or without gathering. Again, we must not subscribe either to biological continuism or to metaphysical separationism (A 52/ATIA 398–399). Indeed, in "And Say the Animal Responded," Derrida says, "if there were a *continuity* between animal and human orders . . . , it would follow [*suivrait*: I will return to the question of following in a moment] this line of evil, of fault and defect" (ASAR 184/136; my emphasis). Here we should also recall Husserl's idea of "analogical appresentation" (where the word "appresentation" renders the German "*Vergegenwärtigung*"). In analogical appresentation, the other is never given as such, never given in a presentation. Based therefore not in the givenness of something as such—in other words, not regulated by the identity of an essence—the staggered analogy is hardly more than a homonym or a catachresis.[8] In other words, we have a comparison between two things that are not completely visible, between two things that are concealed or covered up. So we have to say, then, that Derrida resembles his cat less when he is uncovered and naked; he is most like a cat when he is fully clothed, when he is most uncatlike and most different from a cat. When Derrida is most human, most technological, most concealed, he is most indeterminate, and when he is most indeterminate, when he is only appresented, when he is imperceptible and clandestine, he most resembles a cat. In still other words, Derrida is most catlike when he is most human: when he is writing aporias, he most resembles a cat pacing back and forth before a door, waiting to be let out or to be let in. What is in question here is the analogy of proportion, in which one of the terms of the comparison is determinate, well defined so that it is able to determine the other term.[9] In the staggered analogy, however, both terms are fundamentally indeterminate, which means that the analogy is always a bit off center, inaccurate, and incorrect— in a word, insufficient. When Derrida or you or I, when any of us is most human, we are also most catlike, since we embody traits that can be carried over to cats—or vice versa. So, following this staggered analogy, we have to say that, if I always kind of resemble a cat, I no longer know how to respond to the question I posed to myself under the blind eyes of the other. I am not able to respond to the question of who I am. I am not able to respond, which means that I am also deprived of language just as beasts are. Or, unable to respond, I can respond in countless ways, just as a cat meows in countless ways. We can extend this idea in one more way. If I am unable to respond, if I am only able to react like a cat, then, like a cat again, I am also unable to think. Now we are able to raise the question of what is called not-thinking.

What Is Called Not-Thinking?

"What is called not-thinking?" alludes to Heidegger's *What Is Called Thinking*. There famously, Heidegger says that "what is most thought-provoking is that we are still not thinking." I have constructed a kind of syllogism based on this statement. If animals do not have hands, if they do not speak (and that means that they do not ask and respond to questions), if, even more, animals do not have access to the "as such" of beings (and that means that they do not have access to the world or at least that they are "poor in world"), if they do not die properly or as such (which means that they do not say "ego sum"), then animals do not think. But, if what is most thought-provoking, as Heidegger says, is that we are still not thinking, we humans are thus animals. What is really thought-provoking, then, is that we are animals. But what does us being animals mean? Now, we should recall something from Derrida: "What this animal is, what it will have been, what it would be, what it would like to be, what it could be, this is perhaps what I have been following [*je suis*]" (A 55/ATIA 401). But is Derrida speaking here of animals like cats or of animals like humans? Are we speaking of the ends of man or the ends of animals? I shall return to this question—what could this animal be?—later, but for now I continue with what is called not-thinking.

A variant of Heidegger's "what is called thinking" could be formulated on the basis of the title from Derrida's 1986 "Comment ne pas parler." Instead, we could ask how not to think.[10] In "Comment ne pas parler," Derrida tells us that this question means two things (CNPP 548/15). On the one hand, the phrase tells us to keep quiet, don't speak; it calls for silence. On the other, it calls for speaking; it tells us not to speak badly but rather gives us an injunction to speak well. "How not to think," then, means the same thing. On the one hand, it means not thinking at all (shall we say, not thinking at all like a beast?), and, on the other, it means an injunction to think well. Let us start with thinking well, and in order to do that, I've formulated some slogans, some "mots d'ordres," as we could say in French, some words ordering us to think well of animals, ordering us not to think badly of them.[11] I've constructed four such imperatives.

First, do not think that animals do not suffer. As Derrida says in "The Animal that Therefore I Am (More to Follow)," "'Can they suffer' asks Bentham simply yet so profoundly. Once its protocol is established, the form of this question changes everything" (A 48/ATIA 396). This question takes us precisely to the powerlessness with which we have been concerned throughout.

Just like us, the animals have a fault; being weak, they come to an end. Second, do not think that the end is the end. There is always repetition or, as I might say, coining a term, there is always "refinition," meaning that the end (*finis*) is always in the process of being done again ("re-"); being done over, there is always an "et cetera."[12] No matter how singular an event or a living being is, there is always the repetition of a minimal form, which produces a specter or a ghost. The repetition is quite evident in the French word for ghost, " *revenant.* " Even the singular cat has a name. And, while the cat will come to an end, the name will survive. It will survive as the " *schibboleth* " around which an alliance could be formed. The idea of an alliance brings us to the third imperative for not thinking: Third, do not think in terms of the enemy. If every single other is wholly other, do not think that this complete alterity produces only enemies who must be killed. Friendship suspends the killing, even if this suspension is violently instituted, even if the condition of friendship and peace consists in the ability to kill or be killed (PA 144/122; AAEL 152/85). The fourth imperative does not really follow from the third. It rather encompasses all the imperatives that we could formulate since it concerns the negation in "comment *ne pas* penser." Here is the imperative: Do not think that a negation or a privation is simply a lack. The privation must be conceived as something positive, as a kind of power, but a power that is as well impotent (*impuissance*), a strength that is as well weak, a kind of weak force. We could say that the privation amounts to a power that can be shared (and here we would have to rely on the French verb " *partager,* " which suggests both participation and partitioning). This weak force means that, if we are going to say that animals are deprived of the power of thinking, of responding, and therefore of questioning, this deprivation takes us back to the noise, the meows, the howls but also the songs, the poetry, the silences and gestures that are prior to language, prior, that is, to language in the sense of the apophantic proposition "S is P."[13] Utilizing one of the adverbs of negative theology, we could say that the animals are deprived of questioning without being deprived of it (see CNPP 592/60, also 577/46, 542/8). The use of this adverb would imply that the verb "to question" is lacking, yet the adverb, being right next to the verb, in this place, would imply that the verb lacks only determination. In other words, the adverb would imply that the verb is deprived only of a sense that is proper. Through the adverb "without," the verb becomes a multiplicity; it becomes the infinitive.[14] Lacking only determination, the infinitive indicates a power to think that is in fact more than, larger than, as if it is a container or receptacle, any known form of thinking or questioning; it indicates, we might say, a kind of superthinking. In "And Say the Animal Responded," Derrida complains that Lacan does not provide even anecdotal evidence about animals to support his claims. Here we could provide an anecdote. When the tsunami rolled across the Indian Ocean on December 26, 2005, it is reported that animals fled in advance and (unlike countless humans) were not killed. What kind of thinking took place here on this event?

We have seen that, although the phrase "comment ne pas penser" is a question, within that question, thanks to the negation, we have an imperative; in fact, within that question, we have an imperative to think. Thinking badly about the animals' power to think and speak would be a form of logocentrism. Thinking well about the animals' power would be to think in terms of what Heidegger himself calls "*Zusage*." This term comes from Heidegger's 1957 "The Essence of Language" essay. There he says, "What do we discover when we give sufficient thought to the matter? This, that questioning is not the authentic attitude of thinking, rather it is listening to the *Zusage* of that which must come into question."[15] It is very difficult to translate the German "*Zusage*." In English, it can be rendered as "grant," which is how

Peter D. Hertz renders it in *On the Way to Language*, or it could be rendered as "acquiescence," "affirmation," "agreement," "trust," "confidence," or even "promise." The French translators (Jean Beaufret, Wolfgang Brokmeier, and François Fédier) render it as "fiance," as in "fiancé" and "fiduciary," which connects the term to "promise" (being promised), "faith," and "credit"; in a footnote, the French translators add, "This word says the fact of agreement. In old French, 'fiancier' means 'to commit one's faith.' *Die Zusage* is this original mode of saying or, rather, of the said: the fact that the said (*die Sage*) is said to [*à*] (*zu*) to the human being when strictly nothing other is said to him than the said."[16] Beaufret, Brokmeier, and Fédier are suggesting here that the *Zusage* is language itself speaking of nothing, language having no direct object.

I am pausing at this untranslatable term because of what Derrida says in "The Animal that Therefore I Am (More to Follow)": "the 'moment,' agency and possibility of *Zusage* belong to an 'experience' of language about which one could say that, even if it is not in itself 'animal,' is not lacking [*privé*] in the 'animal.' [Saying that] would be sufficient [*suffirait*] to destabilize a whole tradition [that is, the Cartesian tradition that Derrida think runs from Descartes to Heidegger, and from Kant to Levinas and Lacan], to deprive [this tradition] of its fundamental argument" (ATIA 62 n. 1/407 n. 29). So, even though Heidegger speaks of *Zusage*, we will not be following him. Indeed, this "we cannot follow Heidegger" is what Derrida says in "Faith and Knowledge."

There, in "Faith and Knowledge," Derrida refuses to follow Heidegger when Heidegger says, at the very end of "The Anaximander Fragment," that "faith has no place in thinking" (FS 78/60, paragraph 48).[17] Heidegger, of course, is rejecting faith in the sense of dogmatic belief in authority. But Derrida insists that Heidegger is rejecting "faith in general." It is faith in general that Derrida thinks cannot be dissociated from what Heidegger has called "*Zusage*" (FS 79/60, paragraph 48). As we have just seen, *Zusage* is prior to questioning in Heidegger himself, at least in "The Essence of Language" essay. As Beaufret, Brokmeier, and Fédier suggest, the *Zusage* concerns language speaking about nothing; it suggests, then, Heidegger's famous sentence that "speech speaks" instead of man. In order to be able to question, then, "it is necessary," as Derrida says in *Of Spirit*, "that we *already* be in the element of speech. It is really necessary that, already, speech speaks for us—it must, so to speak, be already spoken and addressed to us" (DLE 147–148 n. 1/129 n. 5; Derrida's emphasis). This "already" or "advance," this priority of speech means that a question, including the question of being, is able to arise only if speech has been given over, that is, entrusted to us. But this entrusting means that the zone of the *Zusage* is a zone of faith. We have to be faithful. Language is entrusted to us, as if we were a mark, a token, a poker chip, a "gage," as Derrida says, that takes the place of the speaking speech, as if we are a supplement. The entrusting means that language is promised to us, and we promise to obey or listen to language. Acquiescence or an affirmation or an agreement is there before any word, which is why Derrida speaks of "this word [the word "yes"] that is at times *without word*" (DLE 148 n. 1/130 n. 5; my emphasis). In other words, the promise of language would be silent. As Derrida says, in "Comment ne pas parler," the discursive event presupposes the open space of the promise (CNPP 545/13). Here one would say, "I have promised to speak of the promise," which implies that the promise is made prior to the speaking of the promise. I am engaged in the promise before any words are spoken, words that would amount to being the keeping of the promise. On the other hand, "this commitment [*engagement*], this word that has been given, already belongs to the time of the *parole* by which 'I keep my word,' or 'tiens parole,' as one says in French" (CNPP 545–46/13). Of course, what Derrida means here is that there are all sorts of ways of keeping a promise, including saying nothing at all. And saying nothing at all would be breaking the promise, too, since it postpones indefinitely the speaking that would keep the promise. We can see here that the *Zusage*, for Derrida, is at once silent and secret, deprived of language and the question and yet engaged in language and the question. The originary jointure or alliance for Derrida is also an originary out-of-jointness and dis-alliance. Wherever there is "Die Sprache spricht," there is also "Die Sprache verspricht sich" (DLE 147/94).[18] The zone of the *Zusage* does not remain unscathed (FS 81/62, paragraph 48). But again we must stress this priority of the *Zusage*, which is the experience of language that is already in common among all living beings; it is the experience of a "we," even a "*Geschlecht*," that includes silence and privation of language. It includes, in other words, marks, as I have said, traces, as in the traces left behind by animals, traces that we could follow.[19]

Derrida gives us a remarkable image of these traces in *Of Spirit*. He calls it "a perverse reading of Heidegger." This reading would follow rigorously and consistently all the instructions that Heidegger gives us to place under erasure or cross through words such as "Being," to cross through the word "spirit," to cross through all the names referring to the beings that do not have *Dasein* (like the animal), and finally to cross through all the question marks since questioning is not what properly defines thinking. Here is what Derrida says: "One can imagine the surface of a text given over to the gnawing, ruminant, and silent voracity of such an animal-machine and its implacable 'logic.' This would not be simply 'without spirit,' it would be a figure of evil" (DLE 152–153 n. 1/134 n. 5). And yet, if we were to see such a text, would we not see there the frenzied crossings and recrossings of animals who were awaiting their end? Would we not see there the traces and remains of their suffering? Would we not see there in this silent voracity a sort of imploration, even a prayer? Prayer is not a constative statement, a proposition in the form of "S is P." Prayer is not concerned with the true and the false; it is not concerned with the "as such" (FS 86/66, paragraph 51). Prayer is not a hymn. Prayers amount to a question of hands. In prayer, the hands are not grasping. The hands are asking for something to be given that they can take; "prier," as Derrida pointed out in "Circumfession," implies "*prendre*" (to take).[20] We might even say that the hands are imploring for forgiveness since the fault is distributed to them, since, always, they have been evil (*mal*), guilty (cf. A 89).[21]

Following, Waiting, Carrying—Rams

On the basis of the analysis I have just completed, we can say that we have not really been thinking. We have not really been questioning language. We have been affirming it; we have been in the zone of faith. But this zone tells us what we should do. We can add the adverb and say that we should not be thinking badly. No, we should think well: it is, once again, undeniable that animals suffer. In "The Animal that Therefore I Am (More to Follow)," Derrida tells us that this thought of undeniability is not "the rock of indubitable certainty, the foundation of every assurance that we could, for example, look for in the *cogito*, in the *Je pense donc je suis*. But from another perspective we are here putting our trust [*fions*] in another agency that is just as radical, although it is essentially different from it: the undeniable" (A 49/ATIA 396). Through the "nous fions," we see that Derrida is referring back to the level of faith. It is from this level of faith or trust that we can say "donc je suis." I have already hinted at this: throughout *L'animal que done je suis*, Derrida plays continuously on the homonymic relation between "être" and "suivre," between "je suis," that is, "I am," and "je suis," that is, "I follow." Minimally, following implies a path, a track, traces. Is it possible for animals in their tracings to lead us astray?

According to Derrida in "And Say the Animal Responded," Lacan does not think so, and this is why Lacan's reflections on animals are, for Derrida, not sufficient.[22] Lacan remains within the Cartesian tradition that the phrase "l'animal que donc je suis" is putting in question. For Lacan, in "The Subversion of the Subject," there is a clear distinction between the animal's strategic pretense, which occurs in pursuit, war, or seduction, and human deception in speech, which is lying (ASAR 175/130).[23] Derrida specifies the idea of deception in speech: "deception involves lying to the extent that, in promising what is true, it includes the supplementary possibility of telling the truth in order to lead the other astray, in order to have him believe something other than what is true" (ASAR 175/130). Even though Lacan admits that animals use lure and dance, "the choreography," as Derrida says, of the hunt and seduction, Lacan denies of them this power to pretend consciously that one is pretending (ASAR 175/130; see also RPS 83/65). We can see already the problem with this Lacanian distinction. It puts humans who are supposed to be subjected to the unconscious on the side of consciousness (we consciously pretend to pretend), while the animals, lacking conscious second-order deception, end up on the side of the unconscious. But the problem with the distinction really lies in the fact that one does not know "in the name of what knowledge or testimony . . . it would be possible to calmly declare that the animal in general is incapable of pretending pretense" (ASAR 182/135). As Derrida notes, "Lacan does not invoke here [in "The Subversion of the Subject"] any ethological knowledge . . . , nor any experience, observation, or personal attestation that would be worthy of credence" (ASAR 183/135). This distinction between animals having only pretense and humans having the pretense of pretense looks to be a dogma. It seems therefore difficult, and

Derrida says that we probably have a feeling that this is so, to determine an indivisible limit between pretense and the pretense of pretense. Indeed, as Derrida points out, pretense presupposes taking the other into account and therefore taking the expectations of the other into account (ASAR 183/136). The pretense of pretense would be there as a necessary possibility, then, as soon as anyone, the animal included, takes the other into account. And no one, including Lacan, would deny that animals take others into account (see A 183/136). Animals perhaps deceive therefore in a deceptive, even human way. Perhaps we have to say that animals even lie and try to keep secrets.[24] Yet, as we have seen, the power to keep secrets is limited. The only way to cover over or efface one's own tracks consists in making more tracks. Erasing a trace can take place only by laying down another trace, which means that one always necessarily leaves a trace of erasure. There is always a specter or a ghost left behind. Like humans, the animals cannot radically erase their own traces; they cannot radically destroy, deny, or put to death their own traces (ASAR 186/138). But this retracing or, more precisely, these retracings also mean that all paths go in multiple directions; there is no one proper sense or direction in the traces. In following the traces therefore, it is always possible that we are deceived; it is always possible that we are going astray.

Following, as we have already noticed in Derrida, is a following of the line or, more precisely, the lines of the fault. As we saw in "Plato's Pharmacy," the fault is a kind of nonplace, a "place of the dead" (*la place du mort*). The phrase "la place du mort" is a term that belongs to the discourse of French structuralism from the 1960s; referring to the dummy hand in bridge, it belongs to structuralism's reflections on games and play. So we must stress that Derrida, in his discussion of "*suivre*" (to follow) in the context of Lacan, repeats something said much earlier by Deleuze in his old (it dates from 1967) essay on structuralism.[25] As I have already suggested with my reference to *psyché* in Foucault, Derrida's thought, including Derrida's very late thought of following in *L'animal que donc je suis*, emanates from the ideas formulated, indeed, invented, by the generation of French philosophers of the sixties, the generation of the incorruptibles. We should note that Lacan's *Ecrits* appeared in the same year as Foucault's *Les mots et les choses*: 1966. In "How Does One Recognize Structuralism," Deleuze defines structure in structuralism as the link between two or more series;[26] the series are unified and differentiated by what he calls "the empty square" (*la case vide*). Deleuze presents Lacan's idea of a partial object, which is never in the place it is supposed to be, as one of the examples of the empty square.[27] I have mentioned Lacan's symbolic before, but what is more important here is that, at the end of his essay, Deleuze speaks of the practice of structuralism. Since the square is empty, we could attempt to fill it completely, either with man or with god. But such a complete occupation is not the practice of structuralism. The structuralist practice consists in "accompanying" the empty square and—this is Deleuze's word—"following" (*suit*) it.[28] Of course, in this essay, Deleuze speaks frequently of Foucault, especially, his *Mots et les choses* (which I just mentioned). We should note that the title Foucault gives to the first chapter of *Les mots et les choses*, the famous analysis of the Velasquez painting, does not correspond with the title normally given to Velasquez's painting, *Las Meninas*. Foucault's title does not even correspond to the French translation of the Spanish title, "Les ménines"; the title of the chapter is "Les suivantes." We could make a bastard English translation of this title as follows; we could say that title is "The Followers." I would be willing to suggest that this bastard translation tells us who we are. But a more normal translation of the phrase "les suivantes" would be "the ladies-in-waiting." This uncontroversial translation gives us a hint of the problem of understanding what following is: following is waiting.

We must now return to "Awaiting (at) the Arrival." I already examined Derrida's interpretation of Heidegger's phrase "Dasein steht bevor sich" in chapter 2. Recall that this phrase concerns standing before oneself in death. Derrida translates "*sich stehen*" in terms of the French reflexive verb "*s'attendre*," and he stresses both the spatial and temporal senses of the German preposition "*bevor*." The preposition means that, in death, I stand "before" myself, earlier, which means that I, me myself, am already out there at the limit of death. If I am already out there, over there and not here, then I have already, earlier, died. If I have already died, then my waiting for myself is late or, more precisely, later; I've missed my rendezvous. With this interpretation, therefore, Derrida transforms the concept of waiting into one of lateness. He transforms the memory of waiting—I remembered my appointment—into forgetting—I'm late because I forgot my appointment. I forgot but I just remembered, which means that I am in a hurry, running to catch up, in a word, following. So, following means running to catch up. The animals that therefore I follow are animals I am urgently trying to reach. Their suffering must be relieved right now. No excuse is possible. Derrida's transformation of the concept of waiting into lateness means that waiting has no alibi. Because you are late, there really is no waiting.

This urgency is why Derrida rejects both the phenomenological concept of horizon and Kantian regulative ideals. In *Rogues* but also in "Force of Law," Derrida argues that the use of Kantian regulative ideals implies nothing more than an ideal possibility that is deferred (FL 57–60/26–27, V 122–23/83–84). The idea of a deferred possibility takes away the sense of urgency that goes along with Derrida's late waiting that follows. To the idea of an infinitely deferred possibility, Derrida opposes all the figures of the impossible, of what must remain in a nonnegative fashion foreign to the order of my possibilities, to the order of "I can," to the order of ipseity. In chapter 2, I also noted the link between possibility and impossibility. The link means that what I am following, what I am waiting for, is impossible, the impossible, the possibility of having no more possibilities, in a word, death. But even more the impossible has already happened, is actually happening. The animal I am following, that I am, has already, is actually turning on me, menacing me, accusing me. As Derrida says in *Rogues*,

> This im-possible is not privative. It is not the inaccessible, and it is not what I can indefinitely send back [*renvoyer*]: it announces itself to me; it precedes me, swoops down upon and seizes me *here now* in a non-virtualizable way, in actuality and not potentiality. It comes upon me on high, in the form of an injunction that does not simply wait on the horizon, that I do not see coming, that never leaves me in peace and never lets me put it off until later. Such an urgency cannot be *idealized* any more than the other as other can. This im-possible is thus not a (regulative) *idea* or (regulating) *ideal*. It is what there is most undeniably *real*. And sensible. Like the other.
>
> (V 123/84; Derrida's emphasis).

Since waiting for the other, whom I am following, does not involve a horizon, the responsibility of what remains to be decided or done (in actuality) cannot consist in following, applying, or carrying out a norm or rule. Having no horizon, this waiting and following are not any sort of program or method. They are not any sort of "camp-following," as Bennington and Bowlby translate "*suivisme*" in *Of Spirit* (DLE 71/44). To follow in the sense of "*suivisme*" is to be a machine, and therefore it involves no responsibility. More precisely, having no horizon—a Kantian regulative ideal always unifies—there is no unity to the possible responses. There can only be dispersion and multiplicity. The animals, in the plural, are everywhere, all around me. I am following them because I am after them, as if they are out ahead of me, in the future. I am following them because I come after them, as if they went ahead of me, died earlier than I. If waiting therefore amounts to not being on time or even to not being early, if waiting amounts to being late for the rendezvous with death, in urgently trying to catch up, then within this reflective structure of death, we must not only speak of an "originary finitude" but an "originary mourning" (AP 75/39).[29] Mourning, as we know from Freud, is the attempt to internalize the dead in me. If waiting in its lateness is mourning, which for Derrida always remains melancholic and unsuccessful, if waiting is mourning, then waiting turns out to be carrying.

While Derrida, of course, frequently uses the verb "*porter*" and its nominative form "*une portée*," which means something like "scope" and makes us think of hands, and we must not forget "*une porte*," a door (cf. AAEL 138/76; CF 83/54)—while Derrida uses all these variations of "*porter*," he explicitly discusses this term in "Rams," which concerns Paul Celan's poetry.[30] Derrida finishes "Rams" by discussing one poem in particular, the one that ends—I quoted this in the introduction—with: "The world is gone, I must carry you." The German is: "Die Welt ist fort, ich muß dich tragen." This line, Derrida suggests, may be a response to the question in the lines before it (B 67/158): "Wo / gegen / rennt er nicht an?" ("In- / to what / does he not charge?" Like Derrida at times, I am making use here of Michael Hamburger's English translation).[31] This question, which, Derrida says, is in the "interro-negative form" (B 65/156), like "comment ne pas parler," refers to a ram mentioned in the stanza immediately before. The ram, "Widder" in German, "*bélier*" in French, signifies not only the animal but also the zodiac sign Aries. As Derrida points out, it refers to the opening stanza ("Vast, glowing vault/with the swarm of/black stars pushing them-/selves out and away"), to the sky and the movement of the constellations charting time and dates. The world is gone, but there is the sky. We are not far away—I'm not sure we have ever been far away—from spacing and anachronism. In any case, it seems to me that Derrida makes three points in his discussion of these final lines. We must pay careful attention to them, since all three contribute to the search for a more sufficient response to animal suffering; all three concern the world gone away (*fort*).

The first point concerns the ram. Here is the stanza (in English) in which the ram appears: "onto a ram's silicified forehead/I brand this image, between/the horns, in which,/in the song of whorls, the/marrow of melted/heart-oceans swells." Derrida interprets the ram not only as Aries but also as the ram of flesh, the sacrificial ram, for example, the one in the Abraham and Isaac story. But, even more, Derrida interprets it as a "battering ram," a ram made of wood (B 64/156). As Derrida says, "there is war." Since the question—"into what does he not charge?"—is in the negative, the question also functions as an accusation, a charge against all those who sacrifice rams, who sacrifice animals. Derrida calls this ram, this charge, "an infinite revolt," "a violent rebellion by all the scapegoats, by all substitutes." He says, "Able to butt in order to attack or to seek revenge, the ram can declare war or respond to sacrifice by protesting in opposition against it. Its burst of indignant incomprehension would not spare anyone or anything in the world. No one in the world is innocent, not even the world itself" (B 65/157). The ram would want to put an end to the common world of men and God, the world in which sacrifice takes place. Here we can even turn the phrase "l'animal que donc je suis" into an insult against us, against us humans who kill and devour other animals (A 143): we are such animals! The ram wants this beastly world to go away, "*fort*"; the sacrifice of animals must stop. The rams say, all the sacrificial animals, all the animals fattened for the slaughter, say "why me." Why is my suffering not alleviated? And, if we wanted, we could appropriate an idea from the general concept of democracy. In democracy, the ruler and the ruled take turns. If we take the word "*revolt*" in the literal sense, then the revolt of animals could be viewed as a change of turns. It has been our turn to rule, the turn of humans, now it is the turn of the animals (V 46/23). Of course, this turn-taking with animals ruling sounds mad, but at the least the idea presents us with a thought experiment concerning equality. At least, this turn-taking makes us think about sharing sovereign power. But let us pass now to the second and third points. Both concern the very last line: "The world is gone, I must carry you."

The most important thing—this is the second point—that Derrida says about this last line is that, since it stands alone in the poem, "isolated, islanded, separated like an aphorism, the sentence no doubt says something essential about absolute solitude" (B 68/158). Here we must recall that, in "The Animal that Therefore I Am (More to Follow)," Derrida stresses that the cat in the story of nakedness is a real cat, a solitary cat, one that stands alone in its singularity (A 20/ATIA 374). The other, for Derrida, is always defined by absolute singularity (B 69/158) or unsubstitutable singularity (A 26/ATIA 378). When the world is gone, over there (*fort*) and not here (not *da*), when the world is perhaps "infinitely inaccessible," then "I must carry *you*, you alone, you alone in me or on me alone" (B 68/158; Derrida's emphasis). Or the verse, as Derrida suggests, may be interpreted in the reverse. When it is necessary to carry you, the world tends to disappear. The disappearance of the world that occurs with this obligation means that there is no mediator between me and the singular you, there is no elsewhere, no earth, no this world or other world, no *the* world that could provide me with an alibi;

there is no ground, foundation, or support (see also V 213/155).[32] Having no alibi, I am all alone. Derrida says, "I am alone in the world [*au monde*] where there is no longer any world" (B 68/158); "I am alone with you, alone to you alone; we are alone: this declaration is also an engagement" (B 69/158). With this word "*engagement*," we must see here an obligation, a pledge, but also the gage, the token, the marker of replacement. But even with replacement, or because of replacement, carrying in Derrida is always the carrying of the one who is singular.

The third point still concerns this last line: "The world is gone, I must carry you." Carrying or *tragen* or *porter* in this last line, according to Derrida, is temporal (B 71–72/159). On the one hand, it speaks of a child, the child to come. "Rams" is one of the few places in which Derrida speaks of natality.[33] As he notes here, the world for a mother pregnant with child seems to go away. The one in her, the one for whom she is waiting, seems to be the only thing that matters. On the other hand, "carrying" speaks of someone who has died in the past, as in a memory that I carry of a loved one. This memory is in me, like the child growing, because of the internalizing work of mourning, but this mourning is never complete. The other remains other, remains singular and inappropriable (B 73–74/160). Or the other who has passed, again just like the child who is to come, is never given as such, never given in a presentation, but only ever in an analogical appresentation (B 76/161). Carrying means holding on to the other while holding oneself back from presentation, or it means guarding the other in mourning while guarding oneself *from* the other by means of melancholy. Here other takes on the sense, again appropriating an idea from the concept of democracy in general, of anyone whatsoever, "quiconque," as Derrida says in *Rogues*, anyone who happens by, "the living being, the cadaver, the phantom" (V 126/86). Yet we cannot understand what this carrying of anyone whatsoever means unless we connect it to the world being gone. At the end of "Rams," Derrida suggests that the "*Fort-sein*" of world in Celan's poem does not answer to any of the categories that Heidegger lays out in relation to the world. Derrida says, "But what would happen if, in our poem, the departure, the *Fort-sein* of the world, in its proper agency, did not answer to any of these theses or categories [found in Heidegger]? What if the *Fort-sein* exceeded them, from a wholly other place? What if it were everything [*tout*], save [*sauf*]" these three categories (B 79/163)? It is neither worldless, nor poor in world, nor world forming, because, we know, the world being gone, this wholly other place, does not gather. Carrying is not gathering.

Conclusion: The "Weak" Response

As I said, we must bear in mind these three points that Derrida makes in relation to the Celan poem in order to determine a more sufficient response to the undeniability of animal suffering. Here are the three points. First, Derrida in "Rams," it seems to me, instructs us to revolt against the world of sacrifice. Second, on the basis of the interpretation of the Celan poem, Derrida describes a structure in which an absolute singularity that is other than me is *in* me. This structure—an absolute singularity that is other than me in me—is what carrying means. So, third, the structure of carrying (*porter* or *tragen*), for Derrida, is not gathering. Why? Because the world is gone (*fort*), elsewhere, it leaves us without the mundane kind of mediation (the kind of mediation suggested by the concept of horizon or Kantian ideals, which would provide a focal point of gathering) in relation to the absolute singularity, it leaves us without alibi in relation to the others. We can specify this "without alibi" in relation to the animals' suffering: having no alibi, we must recognize the urgency that a more sufficient response is required now!

Thus let us consider a first response. I have repeatedly said that any response that relies on biological continuism or metaphysical separationism will be insufficient. But a more specific and obvious response than these two extreme polar responses is imaginable. Can we claim that the idea of animal rights, which would extend human rights to animals, is sufficient? Although, as I have said before, we must support those who assert rights for animals (A 47–48/ATIA 395), it seems to me that the only answer to this question can be no.[34] The response of animal rights is not sufficient. In the dialogue with Roudinesco, Derrida says, "It is too often the case—and I believe this is a fault or a weakness—that a certain concept of the juridical, that of human rights, is reproduced or extended to animals. This leads to naïve positions that one can sympathize with but that are untenable. A certain concept of the human subject, of post-Cartesian human subjectivity, is for the moment at the foundation of the concept of human rights" (DQD 109–110/64–65; see also FL 55/25). Now, in the dialogue with Nancy, "Il faut bien manger," Derrida clarifies the idea of a post-Cartesian human subjectivity (PS 288/273). Post-Cartesian subjectivity consists in a kind of self-relation or autoaffection that "stands in opposition to every other form of self-relation, for example, what one calls the living in general" (PS 288/273).[35] It is this opposition that provides us with rights. But Derrida wants "to put a stop" to this kind of rights (PS 288/273).[36] In regard to this kind of autoaffection, Derrida explicitly speaks of Heidegger and Levinas, *Dasein* in Heidegger and the hostage in Levinas. Derrida thinks that a certain self-identity determines these two concepts, despite their radicality. In Heidegger, Derrida claims, the call of conscience, a call that is other than human, is "denied to the animal"; in Levinas, the other is always the other man (PS 293–94/279; see also G S4 /172).[37] In short, for both, the other that is in me is not inhuman (PS 290–276).[38] What Derrida is saying is that, for both Heidegger and Levinas, the animals are sent away so that I can speak to myself, so that I can speak to myself as another self, as another human. For Heidegger and Levinas, when one hears oneself speak (*s'entendre-parler*), the oneself one hears, even if it is other, is not an animal.[39] Instead of sending myself out, instead of making myself really other, instead of, let us say, experimenting on myself, I substitute the animals. Derrida calls this substitution "the sacrificial structure of subjectivity" (FL 42–43/18–19; A 40/389), but we could just as well call it "the scapegoat structure." The most extreme statement of the sacrificial structure would be that it forms the enclosed globe of subjectivity. A more minimal statement would be that the sacrificial structure, in Heidegger and Levinas, forms a larger enclosure that includes man and the other man or that includes man and god. But this enclosure is still closed—closed to the animals. The sacrificial structure in Heidegger and Levinas is hospitable, but it is not unconditionally hospitable. As Derrida says, the discourses of Heidegger and Levinas "remain profound humanisms *to the extent that they do not sacrifice sacrifice*" (PS 294/279; Derrida's emphasis; also GS4 418/215).[40] Therefore, if we want to find a more sufficient response than the one given by the discourses of Levinas and Heidegger among others, we must sacrifice sacrifice (see also GL 268–69/241).[41] The idea of sacrificial animals like rams, scapegoats killed to purify against evil, this idea, of course, is a religious idea. We must say therefore that our "weak" response is a religious response. Indeed, as we have seen, our today demands a religious response.

I have already appropriated some ideas from Derrida's 1994 essay "Faith and Knowledge." But I must take it up again since it provides his most detailed discussion of religion. There, borrowing a phrase from Bergson, Derrida describes "the two sources of religion." This is what he says, and we need these two "sources" in order to formulate our response:

> What would orient here "in" [*dans*] this desert, without pathway and without inside [*dedans*], would still be the possibility of a *religio* and of a *relegere*, to be sure, but *before* [Derrida's emphasis] the "link" [*lien*] of *religare*, a problematic etymology and doubtless reconstructed, *before* [Derrida's emphasis again] the link between men as such or between man and the divinity of the god. This would also be like the condition of the "link" reduced to its minimal semantic determination: the *halte* of scruple (*religio* [*ligare*: to tie, bind, debt, see FS 48/34 and 50/36–37]), the restraint of shame [*pudeur*], a certain *Verhaltenheit*, of which Heidegger also speaks . . . , the respect, the responsibility of repetition in the wager [*gage*: pledge] of decision or of affirmation (*re-legere* [*legere*: "to harvest, gather, bring together"; see FS 48/34 and 50/36]) which links up with itself in order to link up with the other.
>
> (FS 26/16, paragraph 20)

It seems to me that this is a very important comment. It indicates that Derrida is trying to unclose or "de-close" the connection or link between humans as such and God so that the link is open to others such as animals, to any others whatsoever.[42] He is trying to move us to a level before, earlier than, this link that is humanistic and theistic. This movement indeed means a level that is atheistic (because it is prior to the link between man and God), and that is why, as I shall elaborate in a moment, this religious response is really irreligious. To make this move, Derrida divides the two Latin roots of the word "religion." On the one hand, we have the restraint of shame ("*religio*"), the holding-ourselves-back that makes the link only to oneself; on the other, we have the repetition implied by the gage, by the marker ("*relegere*"). These two roots then refer to what we must call two forces, the force of restraint and the force of repetition. Insofar as one withholds, one is defined by singularity, and insofar as one repeats, one is defined by universality. But this division of the forces, for Derrida, is not a separation. If we separated the two forces, if we separated the force of holding back from the force of repetition, or if we made one force be continuous with the other, the result would be that we would have either all universality or all singularity. This inseparability is "an irrecusable necessity" (AAEL 128/70); one force irresistibly attracts the other. We are powerless before this attraction. We are so weak—this weakness is the fault itself—that we cannot not trace and follow (that is, repeat) and we cannot not retrace and wait (that is, hold back). This necessary linking is not a gathering, and if we call it substitution, "this thinking of substitution," as Derrida says in "A Word of Welcome," "leads us toward a logic that is hardly thinkable, almost unsayable, that of the possible-impossible, the iterability and replaceability of the unique in the very experience of the unique as such" (AAEL 128/70).[43] This thinking of the unique *with* iterability is *not* sacrificial.

So, to say this again, in order to find the least violence, we must sacrifice sacrifice. The sacrifice of sacrifice means that we must unconditionally renounce sovereignty (V 13/xiv), which means that we must renounce power completely and in general (both biopower and sovereign power, to use the Foucaultian distinction). But that renunciation of sovereignty, in short, the renunciation of power in general, means that we are able to renounce, we have the power to be powerless. We cannot keep the sphere or, better, the globe of subjectivity; it opens itself through the necessary repetition to others in autoaffection. Although I am not going to reproduce them now, I must recall the arguments I produced in chapter 2 that necessarily turn autoaffection into heteroaffection. But even these arguments are not suffi-cient.[44] The inability to keep the circle closed—the border is nec-essarily porous; the limit is necessarily divisible—means that we are able to de-close the circle. The inability to keep the border closed results in contradictory consequences, with which we must negotiate. On the one hand, the inability means that, re-versing the inability into an ability to be able, we are able to wel-come others into ourselves. On the other hand, the inability means that, by welcoming, we internalize others, making them the same as us, making them die as other. But the question is: how are we able to welcome and yet guard the alterity of others? *The de-closing of the globe of subjectivity therefore must occur through naming.* In "The Animal That Therefore I Am (More to Follow)," Derrida stresses the biblical story of naming the ani-mals (A 33/ATIA 384). Our naming of the animals, our naming of ourselves, this naming cannot and must not be rejected. The animals must be named, which implies, through the iterability of the linguistic form, that the animals will die; it is "a mortal existence, for, from the moment it has a name, its name survives" (A 26/ATIA 379; also PA 255/229). The naming contains, in other words, the necessary possibility of death. We cannot avoid this evil and violence of naming; we cannot avoid the force of repetition, which, so to speak, puts the animals to death; we can-not stop our hands from grasping. Yet the force of repetition, as I just indicated, is inseparable from the force of holding-back and letting-go. It is the inseparability of these two forces, the force of holding-back and the force of repetition, that allows, however, a "pure singularity" to link up with a "pure singularity" (FS 26/16, paragraph 20). Although this may be un-Derridean, here I am prioritizing the force of singularity over the force of it-erability. Because of the emphasis of singularity, this structure is not a structure of sacrifice but a structure of saving by means of replacement (cf. V 15/xv, 160/114). The structure of replacement that I am trying to describe here extends what Derrida describes in "Schibboleth for Paul Celan" as the structure of the date. A date is singular, and yet it is remembered. Here we can recall that Derrida dates his postcards collected in *The Post Card*; on the 10th of June 1977, he writes, "we are the worst criminals in history" (PC 38–39/32–33). Or we can think of the 28th of November 1947, when, according to Deleuze and Guattari, Artaud declared war on the organs.[45] Or, following Derrida, we can recall Celan speaking of the 20th of January when Lenz, in Büchner's novella, walks in the mountains (SPC 25/11).[46] As remembered, a date is sent out to (*à*), but not to an eventless repetition; instead, it is sent out to another 20th of January in another year (SPC 21/8).[47] The waiting for the next date is a waiting for another event. Although the date betrays the date through its iterability, its structure of sending to makes no compromise, makes no deal, with the date to come (SPC 22/8). The essential structure of a date, as an event, does not allow itself to pass into eventless repetition. A singular date calls for a singular date; the date to come must be an event, which is singular. As Derrida says in "Schibboleth," "Only another singularity, just as irreplaceable, can take its place *without substituting for it*" (SPC 31/14; my emphasis).

Dating resembles enumeration. It is still a question of numbers. Enumeration must be done. Yet to enumerate is to universalize. Numbers (or, more generally, mathematics, ideal objects) at the limit or virtually are translatable without remainder. Singularity is only captured, not protected by a number. Moreover, as Bergson showed a long time ago, numbers refer to spatially separated coordinates. A singularity, however, is not individuated by spatial separation. I have already referred to the idea of "*espacement*." A singularity is inseparable from iterability, as in the nontotalizing idea of the *khōra*. He or she (we must always worry about the gender of an animal) cannot be gathered together into a one, into the one on which enumeration depends.

There is no unity here; an animal does not appear as such. Unlike a number (the number, for instance, that is given to the animal in order to reduce it to the accountability of a piece of stock, "*Bestand*," as Heidegger would say, "standing reserve"),[48] a date works. It contains unforeseeable events, which, once again, means that a date never appears as such. Not appearing as such, an animal exists only in dispersion. And if an animal exists only in dispersion, then when we kill one, we really don't know how many are killed. How many does it take to make a genocide? Perhaps one alone. What sort of enumeration is required when we must say each time the end of the world in which there are innumerable others?

Like a date, a name is a marker for a singularity. It replaces animals, a name in the place of the animals. But the name must also imply that the animal is singular, even absolutely or purely singular, a singularity for which there can be no substitute (DM 41/41). We would compromise with the singularity of the animals (with the singularity of all others), if the naming of them, if the names for them were only universal, were only general nouns. We would have only sacrifice and substitution, if we only ever spoke of the animal in general (or the enemy in general). Minimally, as Derrida instructs in "The Animal that Therefore I Am (More to Follow)," we must always say "the animals" in the plural (A 53/ATIA 399).[49] Like *khōra*, the animals must always be called in the same way. Before I take the next step, we must remind ourselves of what Derrida says in "Il faut bien manger": "responsibility carries within it, and it must do so, an essential excessiveness [*une démesure essentielle*]" (PS 28/272). This excessiveness means that we must up the ante (*surenchère*) (FL 19–20/44). We must be supererogatory. Like the worst, the least violence is still a question of numbers. But, at infinity, it is a question of the innumerable. It is this excessiveness, it is this being out of all measure that I want to remind you of. So, at the limit, I think,

Derrida is even arguing, or at least this is what I am arguing: we must name all the animals with proper names, eliding all the definite articles (cf. K 31/96–97). Unconditionally, we must name properly each and every one of them, and to name them properly we must call them as they call themselves.[50] This proper nomination is the only way for us to change our relation to them into one of friendship. As Derrida says in *The Politics of Friendship*, "the question of the proper name is obviously at the heart of the friendship problematic. . . . We have a real problem thinking friendship without the proper name" (PA 281/251). Or, more strongly, as he says in "The Deaths of Roland Barthes," "the proper name would have been sufficient" (CF 59/34). The name, simply, is necessary (SN 79–80/68). What sort of name? I have just suggested the proper name. Earlier I mentioned shibboleths. Appropriating some of Derrida's titles, we could say that the names for the animals resemble the "schibboleth for Paul Celan," for the absolutely singular, in this case, a person called with the proper name "Paul Celan"; or we could say they are "memoires for Paul De Man." Another way to think of these names is to conceive them as idioms that are untranslatable (AAEL 205/119).[51] We can go farther: we could speak of homonyms or catachreses or perhaps metonyms, a part for a whole (CF 90/60). Still minimally, eliding the definite articles, we must—here we would be following Deleuze and Guattari—use the indefinite article; instead of "the ram," we say "a ram," instead of "the one god," we say "a god" (V 156/110).[52] The indefinite article, "a" or "one," moves us closer to singularity. This demand or commandment that all the animals, all the others be given names is rational, of course, if we accept that each animal is singular. And yet it is a sort of mad rationality; it is, as Kierkegaard would say, beyond the ethical, beyond universal duty (cf. DM 64/64). By means of giving the animals nonuniversal names, we cannot simply forget all the others whom we are following or, for that matter, simply remember since we have at the end only the names. In sacrifice, in contrast, the substitute is either completely forgotten—any single ram could be sacrificed—or completely remembered—this one alone is the only one. I think that it is only through something like a date (which commemorates an event that has passed away and still to come), only through something like a nonuniversal name that the link, the "*re-legere*," the being-with, the living-together with the animals can be formed. Only in this way is compassion possible. Sacrificing the scapegoat closes this link in order to institute the unscathed link between man and man or between man and god; sacrificing is simply too safe (V 160/114).[53] Only in this way, through the name, can we welcome, make a place for the animals, internalize them, even eat them. You have to eat, after all, as the French expression "il faut bien manger" implies. But this replacement, which does not sacrifice, would be a way of eating the animals *well* ("il faut manger *bien*"). Here, through the specific internalization of the name (and not the flesh of the animals), we are able (as I anticipated in the preface) to advocate a kind of vegetarianism that is compatible with a minimal carnivorism, but what I am really advocating is a kind of asceticism.[54]

Through nonuniversal names, we can keep the globe of subjectivity open. In fact, we cannot keep the animals out. This is our weakness but also our power. Through this weakness, we are able to let more of them and more of us come in. It is still a question of numbers. Letting them in, we are contaminated by them. The contamination by others requires that we change our proper name, making it improper just as Abram's name is changed to "Abraham."[55] But, with our names changed, which signifies the welcome, by replacing them (not sacrificing them), by placing them in us, we are able also not to reciprocate the contamination. We pass now to the other weak force. We are also able to be unable not to retreat, we are able to be unable to hold ourselves back, to let our prehensile organs no longer grasp, to step back and away from the animals, from all the others.[56] This halt is the "*religio*" of the religious response. Keeping ourselves back, we are able to be contaminated by them without being able to make contact with them. We are a bit staggered in relation to them, preserving their singularity, preserving their silence. In relation to this silence, the proper names we use, any name we give to any animal, like the name *khōra*, is always anachronistic and insufficient to their silence since it is a word and not silent, since the word reduces indetermination. To name properly is a kind of violence (DLG 164–165/112). It is also necessary to eat the good, make it the same, make it evil: "Il faut aussi manger le bien." This violence of the proper name is probably why Derrida does not tell us, in *L'animal que donc je suis*, the proper name of his singular cat; it remains a secret. This insufficiency of the proper name is the fault contained in all names (ECM 199/44–45). We must receive the animals through the name, which means that we receive them without really receiving them.

The "without receiving them" contains several implications. As I just stated, we must receive them through the name, which is a kind of violence. But the reception through the name also means that we have no immediate access to the animals themselves. The mediation of the name also protects them at the same time as it violates their alterity. To receive without receiving means that we receive not them, not them themselves, but only their names, only this medium of sameness. Since we are able only to receive the name and not the animal itself, we are able to allow the animals to slip away from any essential determination indicated by the phrase "the animal as such." The mediation of the name implies that, since we never receive the essence of the animal, we are not able to know how many animals are entering. The name is always indefinite, and therefore it is open to pluralization, to multiplicity; we also say "rams" in the plural (how many?), instead of "the animal." The names never, therefore, hit the one true animal in its nakedness; the names are always improper. We are able then to let the animals remain without determination; indeed, lacking an essence, each animal would form a point of resistance to propriety and determination. In their singularity, protected by the mediation of their names, they are even invisible, which allows them to run free, to move in all directions. Echoing Heidegger, who appropriates Hölderlin, we can say that "the animals are signs deprived of sense," meaning that they are without direction, without destination, without "*sens*" or "*Sinn*" in the literal sense. This replacement, this placing of them in us while we hold back would be a kind of misplacement. Where are they? Hidden by the name, we cannot find them in their nakedness. We cannot completely capture them, which would be the kind of freedom that allows them to have a nomadic existence. And, if, after naming the animals, we ate their bodies, their flesh, their meat, in other words, if we did more than internalize them through the name, if we really ate the animals, how could we not suffer from bad conscience?[57] We would suffer from a feeling that our hospitality was insufficient, an insufficiency that that would motivate us to eat better, with a tendency toward the least violence.

We have just seen that the phrase "to receive without receiving" means that the name violates and at the same time protects the animals. To receive without receiving, however, has a second implication. We are not able *not* to receive the animals, which means that they are able to enter without invitation. Reversing the privative "not able" into a positive ability to be unable, we are able then to receive them without invitation. To receive without receiving means that they *must* come in without any invitation. If we really received them, if we received them with receiving, this reception would occur by inviting them in. But, if we invited them, we would make them suffer the conditions that we determine, in other words, we would make them be completely the same as ourselves. Instead, since we are unable to keep them out, we are able to receive them without asking anything of them. We are able not to ask for their papers, we are able to make no judgment of them, we are able not to evaluate. In fact, when they enter, we are able to smile and offer forgiveness, even if the animals, these beasts, have tended toward the worst violence.[58] Since we are unable not to receive them, we are able to affirm the worst and the best chances—in us.[59] The affirmation of them in us therefore would be a kind of peace without peace. This peace would be "without peace" because their coming into us does violence to us and our naming them will do violence to them. There is always suffering; there is always an ordeal. But this peaceful violence is still less; it is not the worst violence. Peace without peace is still peace; it is not war by other means. With this door open, sharing happens. Perhaps, *mondialisation* (not globalization) is happening. And if we have to speak of the enemy here, at the least—we are still seeking the least violent response—the enemy would have a name, which would distinguish him or her or them from all the others. At the least, it would not be the case that every single other would be the enemy.

The structure of replacement that I have just described, which is based on the idea of the date, is difficult and complicated. I would now like to simplify it and make it a little easier. With this idea of the least violence, with this idea of a more sufficient response, what I am trying to do (and I think this is something that Derrida himself has not done) is occupy a space between undecidability and prescription. I am trying to occupy a space between saying almost nothing (at times, undecidability sounds to me when uttered by "Derrideans" like a *flatus voci*) and saying

too much (laws for the treatment of animals, laws of vegetarianism, for example). I do not know if this space in between exists.
But what I have done is construct a kind of "recipe"—how can
we eat *well*, that is, in the least evil way?—for the more sufficient
response. The "recipe" is a bet on human psychology as it is
viewed by common opinion. The central idea lies in the naming
of the animals, which metaphorically "eats" them; naming each
and every one of them (naming as we do a child who is coming)[60] will engage our passions, will make us feel differently, and
our passions will make us think differently and act differently;
naming them, the hope is, will change the way we "literally"
treat and eat the animals.[61] Here is the "recipe" in seven steps.

1. Recognize that we are composed of one force, the force
that does not have the ability or the force to keep the others out.
The definition of a weak force is an ability to be unable, here, an
ability to be unable to hold the others out. In other words, make
the passive active. Let the others in their singularity in.

2. Then, up the ante on this weak force, make it unconditional, which amounts to letting every single other in. Once
again, the more sufficient response is the friendly response: unconditional friendship. And unconditional friendship is unconditional forgiveness since all the others, all the animals, are defective. (We should not forget here that unconditionality follows
from Kant's insight that a law, if it is to be worthy of its name,
requires it to be absolutely universal.)

3. Now, name every single other in its singularity. The name
always results in the iterability of the singular.[62] The iterability is
the same weak force with which we began: letting them in reduces them to a medium of sameness. The medium of sameness
means that I have the ability to be unable to remain silent. The
naming places every single other in a medium that tends toward

universality, in a medium that does violence to that singularity, that even "kills" them in their singularity. The name, so to speak, "eats" them.

4. Recognize, however, that the violence of the name must be done in a certain way. Recognize, in other words, that the animals must be eaten well, with the least amount of violence. How?

5. Carry the name, not the singular other; show restraint. This step back is the other weak force: I am unable not to hold myself back in my singularity, therefore I am able to be unable to be unscathed, which means that I am able not to touch them. So, let them be protected by the name, by the proper name, by the idiom, by the catachresis, by the metonymy. In other words, recognize that the name is a kind of shield that allows animals to be left alone.

6. Recognize that this "recipe" is not sufficient (although it is necessary). The more sufficient response is still not sufficient because there is still suffering, necessarily. The animals are still eaten either "metaphorically" or "literally"; you have to eat, after all. The insufficiency brings us to the seventh and final step.

7. Always feel compassion for the others who are suffering. Have passion with them (com-passion), which means that you must recognize that the animals, all the others, have fear in the face of death (not anxiety), since death always comes from the others, from me or you or us or them.[63]

What this "recipe" describes is an experiment or a test. Following the structure of anti-Platonism that I laid out in chapter 1, it amounts to a reversal. Let us try to reverse unconditional inhospitality, the worst, into unconditional hospitality. Unconditional hospitality is not the best but only the less bad. Indeed, it is a kind of mirror image of the worst. By being vulnerable in the way I have described, there is no guarantee that the worst will be avoided. The recipe describes a dangerous experiment; prudence is required. As mentioned in passing in the recipe, unconditional hospitality takes up the Kantian insight that the law must have the form of universality; it must be applied equally or univocally to everyone no matter who or what. And here we must not overlook the fact that what Derrida has called deconstruction maintains a deep alliance to the Western idea of enlightenment, even as it draws inspiration from one of the voices of Christianity, the voice of weakness.

Even with this appeal to the Kantian or enlightened insight concerning the form of the law, we still have a kind of mirror image. The worst (unconditional nonhospitality) is also the weak response.[64] I am too weak to keep the border closed, I am too weak to keep the other living beings out, and they contaminate me. In the worst, every single living being turns into an evil being, except one, me, man; only one is good. But at the limit in the worst, all living beings are evil, and all universally must therefore—this is an important "therefore"—be destroyed. In the reversal, the weak response turns out to be the strong response since I have the power to let the other living beings in. In the reversal, evil is affirmed; the fault, which seemed to be a property of man alone, is distributed to all living beings (but the limit between living and nonliving is, as Derrida would say, porous); none of them universally is perfect like mechanisms are. In the reversal of the worst into the least bad, all living beings are still evil. The reversal, then, is an experimentation on the equality of violence, which means that all living beings, no matter how violent, are treated equally in the sense of hospitality: all are welcome. Unconditional hospitality is forgiveness. We could say at this moment, "Oh my enemies, there are no enemies." Yet hospitality and equality here do not really function as values; they are instead what I would call "prevalues," valuationally indeterminate. If every single living being, including me, is evil, if every single living being abuses power, then it is not possible to decide which one is more deserving of forgiveness. Is it the one who most abuses power or the one who abuses it the least? And yet it is not possible to welcome every single living being no matter what, unconditionally. There are always conditions; this is a fact, a "*Faktum*" or archifact, something always already made or done (taking the word "fact" in the literal sense of something made). When one ups the ante on hospitality—this "upping of the ante" is also the central idea of the "recipe"—in the face of these factual conditions, then one is forced to a decision and make a valuation, which will have the effect of excluding. Perhaps, *mondialisation* is *not* happening. There are still more living beings who demand forgiveness.

We could say that the weak response I have just formulated (abbreviated in the "recipe"), by the very name of weakness, the very response I have formulated with Derrida's thinking, is a Christian response. As Paul says, "when I am weak, then I am strong" (2 Corinthians 12:12).[65] The response belongs, as Derrida would say, to one of the voices of Christianity.[66] We see this Christian response in the imagined dialogue between Heidegger and a Christian theologian that Derrida writes in *Of Spirit* (DLE 178/109). We see this especially in *Rogues*. There Derrida wonders—imploring, I think, Europe but also the West in general, imploring probably and especially the United States—whether "a Christian democracy, more than any other, more than social democracy or popular democracy, [would] be welcoming to the enemies of democracies [we might call these enemies of democracy "uncivilized animals"]; [a Christian democracy] should turn the other cheek, offer hospitality, grant freedom of expression and the right to vote to antidemocrats" (V 66/41). Our more sufficient response, then, our religious response, would seem to be Christian. But this is not entirely true. We have seen that the link precedes the link before man and God. The response is therefore irreligious. In fact, I think we have to say that Derrida, perhaps throughout his entire career (cf. DLE 178/108–09), was involved in what Nancy has called a "deconstruction of Christianity," a deconstruction that would aim to designate, within Christianity, an "arche," a beginning, a "provenance" of Christianity (and therefore of the West) that is "more profound than Christianity itself."[67] In other words, it would be a provenance that is not Christian.[68]

So, what Derrida is really leading us toward is not Christian negative theology. I would say instead that he is leading toward the Greek *khōra*. The idea of replacement, which limits the violence of substitution, concerns the spacing that only the *khōra* makes available. In "Comment ne pas parler," Derrida stresses that the *khōra* is no god, it makes no promise, and no prayer can be addressed to it (CNPP 570/39). Even as it gives and receives, it withholds itself. With globalization, the world may be in us (which means that it is no longer the world), but we are in the *khōra*. The *khōra* is the world gone away, infinitely inaccessible, providing no foundation. And, if there is a promise, it is the promise that I make to you, that all of us make to all of you: I *must* carry you. Yet Derrida does not stop with the Greek *khōra*, as if that were sufficient. Again in "Comment ne pas parler," Derrida allies the thought of the *khōra* with the God of Christian negative theology because Dionysius the Aeropagite compares divine participation to the seal and wax, just as Plato compares the *khōra* to a piece of wax (CNPP 582.50–51). The piece of wax, however, takes us back to one of Derrida's earliest examinations, his examination in 1966 of the magical writing pad in Freud (ED 334/226). Perhaps here we have to say that the provenance of Christianity resides in the idea of the "jewgreek" that Derrida mentions, quoting Joyce, at the end of "Violence and Metaphysics" (ED 228/153). Perhaps. In any case, as Freud describes it, the magic writing pad allows one to write or better trace something on a wax tablet but through a cellophane sheet; then, by lifting the cellophane sheet, one is able to erase those traces, allowing one to trace again and over what was at first written. Like *khōra*, the wax tablet at the back of the pad receives the imprints while remaining virginal, receives the imprints while giving over the space for the tracings. And, just as there are two sources of religion, there are two inseparable forces with the magic pad: the force of tracing and the force of erasing. As Derrida says, the magic pad, which he calls a machine, "does not run by itself. . . . And it is not held with only one hand. . . . At least two hands are needed to make the apparatus function" (ED 334/226). Of course, when Derrida says, "at least two hands," this comment means there could be more than two hands. But if there are more than two hands, they are no longer hands; we have to imagine paws or feelers, even "antennae" (ED 333/225). If the magic writing pad is really a model for repression, even more generally a model for the unconscious, then no other conclusion is possible than that therefore I am an animal. Does this conclusion finally lead us to think well of animals since they are in us as the unconscious? Does this thinking well of the animals provide a more sufficient response to animal suffering? No, animals are not even the unconscious, not even the id, not even "*ça*." No, they are not even "that" (*ça* again).[69] This final denial opens up the question that I raised earlier: who are we? I have suggested that we must think of ourselves as followers, but we must also think of ourselves, us humans, as the incorruptibles. And therefore, if we want to be most human, the most humane, we must let ourselves be corrupted in countless ways, by countless others.

The Generation of the Incorruptibles

"Freud and the Scene of Writing," in which Derrida examines Freud's magic writing pad, appeared for the first time in 1966, and it was collected in *Writing and Difference* which appeared in 1967, alongside of *Voice and Phenomenon* and *Of Grammatology*. At this time, other great books appeared. I have already mentioned Foucault's *Les mots et les choses* (*The Order of Things* is the English-language title), which appeared in 1966. Deleuze's *Difference and Repetition* was published in 1968. It is hard to deny that the philosophy publications of this epoch indicate that we have before us a kind of philosophical moment (a moment perhaps comparable to the moment of German idealism at the beginning of the nineteenth century). Hélène Cixous calls this generation of French philosophers (that includes as well Lyotard) "the incorruptibles." In the last interview, Derrida gave (it was to *Le Monde* during the summer of 2004), he provided an interpretation of "the incorruptibles": "By means of metonymy, I call this approach [of "the incorruptibles"] an intransigent, even incorruptible, *ethos* of writing and thinking . . . , without concession even to philosophy, and not letting public opinion, the media, or the phantasm of an intimidating readership frighten or force us into simplifying or repressing. Hence the strict taste for refinement, paradox, and aporia." Derrida proclaims that today, more than ever, "this predilection [for paradox and aporia] remains a requirement." How are we to understand this requirement, this predilection for "refinement, paradox, and aporia" (the literal meaning of these last two words must be kept in mind: "paradoxa," against *doxa* or common opinion, and "aporia," the inability to cross a line, an impasse)?

In "Typewriter Ribbon" from 1998, Derrida investigates the relation of confession to archives. But, before he starts the investigation (which will concern primarily Rousseau), he says, "Let us put in place the premises of our question." Before we turn to these premises, we must recall that Derrida, in *Rogues*, says that we must be "responsible guardians of the heritage of transcendental idealism" (V 188/134). We are able to discover these premises only through transcendental idealism. Therefore, in "Typewriter Ribbon," Derrida says, "Will this be possible for us? Will we one day be able to, and in a single gesture, to join the thinking of the event to the thinking of the machine? Will we be able to think, what is called thinking, at one and the same time, both what is happening (we call that an event) and the calculable programming of an automatic repetition (we call that a machine). For that, it would be necessary in the future (but there will be no future except on this condition) to think both the event and the machine as two compatible or even in-dissociable concepts. Today they appear to us to be antinomic" (RME 34/72). These two concepts appear to us to be antinomic because we conceive an event as something singular and nonrepeatable. Moreover, as I have discussed, Derrida associates this singularity to the living. The living being undergoes an affection, and this affection gets inscribed in organic material. The idea of an inscription leads Derrida to the other pole. The machine that inscribes is based in repetition; "It is destined, that is, to reproduce impassively, imperceptibly, without organ or organicity, the received commands. In a state of anaesthesis, it would obey or command a calculable program without affect or auto-affection, like an indifferent automaton" (RME 35/72). The automaticity of the inorganic machine is not the spontaneity attributed to organic life. It is easy to see the incompatibility of the two concepts: organic, living singularity (the event) and inorganic, dead universality (mechanical repetition). Derrida says that, if we can make these two concepts compatible, "you can bet not only (and I insist on not only) will one have produced a new logic, an unheard-of conceptual form. In truth, against the background and at the horizon of our present possibilities, this new figure would resemble a monster." The monstrosity of this paradox between event and repetition announces, perhaps, another kind of thinking, an impossible thinking: the impossible event (there must be resemblance to the past that cancels the singularity of the event) and the only possible event (since any event to be so must be singular and nonresembling). Derrida concludes this discussion by saying: "To give up neither the event nor the machine, to subordinate neither one to the other, neither to reduce one to the other: this is perhaps a concern of thinking that has kept a certain number of 'us' working for the last few decades" (RME 37/74). This "us" refers to Derrida's generation of thinkers: "the incorruptibles."

Clearly, Cixous intends with this word to imply that the generation of French philosophers who came of age in the sixties, what they wrote and did, will never decay, will remain endlessly new and interesting. This generation will remain pure. But the term is particularly appropriate for Derrida, since his thought concerns precisely the idea of contamination (see LI 146/78). On the basis of the pharmakon, we have seen that contamination, in Derrida, implies that an opposition consisting in two pure poles separated by an indivisible line never exists; instead, one term always and necessarily "infects" the other. Nevertheless, for Derrida, a kind of purity remains as a value. In his 1992 *The Monolingualism of the Other*, Derrida speaks of his "shameful intolerance" for anything but the purity of the French language:

> I still do not dare admit this compulsive demand for a purity of language except within boundaries of which I can be sure: this demand is neither ethical, political, nor social. It does not inspire any judgment in me. It simply exposes me to suffering when someone, who can be myself, happens to fall short of it. I suffer even further when I catch myself [*surprend*] or am caught "red-handed" [*pris*] in the act. . . . Above all, this demand remains so inflexible that it sometimes goes beyond the grammatical point of view, it even neglects "style" in order to bow to a more hidden rule, to "listen" to the domineering murmur of an order which someone in me flatters himself to understand, even in situations where he would be the only one to do so, in a tête-à-tête with the idiom, the final target: a last will of the language, in sum, a law of the language that would entrust itself only to me. . . . I therefore admit to a purity which is not very pure. Anything but a purism. It is, at least, the only impure "purity" for which I dare confess a taste.   (MLA 78–79/46)

Derrida's taste for purity is such that he seeks the idioms of a language. The idioms of a language are what make the language singular. An idiom is so pure that we seem unable to translate it out of that language. Derrida, we have seen, always connects the French idiom "il faut," "it is necessary," to "une faute," "a fault," and to "un défaut," "a defect," but we cannot make this connection between necessity and a fault in English. This idiom seems to belong alone to French; it seems as though it cannot be shared; so far, there is no babble of several languages in the sole French language. And yet, even within one language, an idiom can be shared. Here is another French idiom: "il y va d'un certain pas" which can be found in *Aporias*. Even in French, this idiom can be translated. On the one hand, if one takes the "il y va" literally, one has a sentence about movement to a place ("y") at a certain pace ("un certain pas": step). On the other hand, if one takes the "il y va" figuratively, one has a sentence (perhaps more philosophical) about the issue of negation ("un certain pas": "a certain kind of not"). This undecidability indicates that, already in the French, in the one French language, there is already translation and, as Derrida would say, "Babelization," "internal minorities."[1] Here we can see that what is most pure in a language, in the *logos*, the pharmakon, for Derrida, is the very possibility of impurity.[2] And this idea of the link between purity and impurity gives us here at the conclusion a way of thinking of ourselves, of being human, of human life. We are not continuous with animals, and we are not separate from them. If we want to be the most human, we must be the most purely human; we must be incorruptible, we must be of the generation (the *Geschlecht*) of the incorruptibles. But then, to be of the generation of the incorruptibles, we must be corruptible in countless ways, in all the ways possible. Being infinitely corruptible limits the worst violence with the least violence: every single other is wholly other *and* every single other corrupts us without being rejected. Every single other is received without being captured. This least violence is what is required for our today so that there might be a tomorrow.

NOTES

Introduction

1. I might add here a "once again." See Leonard Lawlor, *Imagination and Chance: The Difference Between the Thought of Ricœur and Derrida* (Albany: SUNY Press, 1992); and idem, *Derrida and Husserl: The Basic Problem of Phenomenology* (Bloomington: Indiana University Press, 2002).

2. In regard to the machinelike character of animals, the ideas found in Donna Haraway's "A Manifesto for Cyborgs: Science, Technology, and Socialist Feminism in the 1980's" could be integrated into what I am saying here, in particular, the idea that cyborgs do not "seek unitary identity" and Haraway's claim that "the machine is us," which could be translated into French as "l'animal que donc je suis." See Donna Haraway's "A Manifesto for Cyborgs: Science, Technology, and Socialist Feminism in the 1980's," in *The Haraway Reader* (London: Routledge, 2004), p. 38.

3. I will use this French title whenever I am referring to material that has not yet been translated into English, that is, chapters 2 and 4.

4. Peter Singer, *Animal Liberation* (New York: HarperCollins, 2002 [1975]). This claim does not mean that I think Derrida would subscribe to the sociobiology or naturalism in Singer's *The Expanding Circle: Ethics and Sociobiology* (New York: Farrar, Strauss and Gir-

oux, 1981) (see especially the first chapter). Singer, however, says that, for him, the term "gene" "does not refer to the physical bits of DNA—which cannot survive any longer than the individual wolf, blackbird, or human in which they are present—but to the type of DNA." An examination of the idea of type here could lead in a very different direction from sociobiology.

5. Singer, *Animal Liberation*, p. 7.
6. Ibid., p. 8. See also Tom Regan's discussion of Singer in *The Case for Animal Rights* (Berkeley: University of California Press, 1985), pp. 206–231.
7. See especially Henry Spira and Peter Singer, "Ten Points for Activists," in *In Defense of Animals: The Second Wave*, ed. Peter Singer (Oxford: Blackwell, 2006), pp. 214–224.
8. Because we must necessarily internalize the other, I am certain that it is not possible, in principle and in fact, to remain entirely unscathed by carnivorousness. In "Faith and Knowledge," Derrida says, "It is always the sacrifice of the living [*vivant*], more than ever in large-scale breeding and slaughtering, in the hunting and fishing industries, in animal experimentation. Be it said in passing that certain ecologist and certain vegetarians—at least to the extent that they believe themselves to have remained pure of (unscathed by) all carnivorousness, even symbolic—would be the only 'religious' persons of the time to respect one of these two pure sources of religion and indeed to bear [*porter*] responsibility for what could be the future of a religion" (FS 67–68/50). For asceticism, see Henri Bergson, *Les deux sources de la morale et de la religion*, in *Œuvres* (Paris: Presses Universitaires de France, 1959), p. 1238; idem, *The Two Sources of Morality and Religion*, trans. R. Ashley Audra and Cloudesley Brereton with the assistance of W. Horsfall Carter (Notre Dame: University of Notre Dame Press, 1977 [1935]), p. 308. See also my *The Challenge of Bergsonism: Phenomenology, Ontology, Ethics* (London: Continuum, 2003), pp. 91–96.
9. Gilles Deleuze and Félix Guattari, *Qu'est-ce que la philosophie* (Paris: Minuit, 1991), p. 36; idem, *What Is Philosophy*, trans. Graham Burchell (New York: Columbia University Press, 1994), pp. 32–33.
10. Jean-Luc Nancy, *Déconstruction du christianisme*, vol. 1, *La déclosion* (Paris: Galilée, 2005), p. 229.

11. See also LI 174/93: "Although this 'exigency' [the metaphysical exigency for an origin that is simple] is here essentially 'idealistic' I do not criticize it as such, but rather ask myself what this idealism is, what its force and its necessity are, and where its intrinsic limit is to be found. Nor is this idealism the exclusive property of those systems commonly designated as 'idealistic.' It can be found at times in philosophies that proclaim themselves to be anti-idealistic, in 'materialisms.'"

12. See Deleuze and Guattari, *Qu'est-ce que la philosophie*, especially p. 50; and *What Is Philosophy*, pp. 48–49. Here, Deleuze and Guattari say,

> This plane [of immanence] presents two sides to us, extension and thought, or rather its two powers, power of being and power of thinking. Spinoza is the vertigo of immanence from which so many philosophers try in vain to escape. Will we ever be mature enough for a Spinozist inspiration? It happened once with Bergson: the beginning of *Matter and Memory* marks out a plane that slices through the chaos—both the infinite movement of matter that continually propagates itself, and the image of a thought that everywhere continually spreads an in principle pure consciousness (immanence is not immanent "to" consciousness but the other way around).

> Even if Deleuze speak of "transcendental empiricism" rather than "transcendental idealism," what is important is the idea of a transcendental experience.

13. Deleuze and Guattari also use this adverb. See *Capitalisme et schizophrénie 2: Mille plateaux* (Paris: Minuit, 1980), p. 110; *A Thousand Plateaus*, trans. Brian Massumi (Minneapolis: University of Minnesota Press, 1987), p. 87. Massumi translates "à même" as "on the same level."

14. See Nancy, *La déclosion*. See also Jean-Luc Nancy, "La deconstruction du christianisme," in *Les Études Philosophiques*, no. 4 (1998): 503–519; idem, "The Deconstruction of Christianity," trans. Simon Sparks, in *Religion and Media*, ed. Hent De Vries and Samuel Weber (Stanford, Calif.: Stanford University Press, 2001), pp. 112–130. ✓

15. Martin Heidegger, *Kant und das Problem der Metaphysik* (Frankfurt am Main: Klostermann, 1973 [1929]), pp. 188–195; idem, *Kant and*

the Problem of Metaphysics, trans. Richard Taft (Bloomington: Indiana University Press, 1990), pp. 129–133.

16. See Michel Foucault, *La naissance de la clinique* (Paris: Presses Universitaires de France, 1997 [1963]), p. 148; idem, *The Birth of the Clinic*, trans. A. M. Sheridan Smith (New York: Vintage, 1994), p. 145. Derrida also stresses this connection of mortalism and vitalism in Foucault's *Birth of the Clinic* (which occurs in Foucault's study of Bichat). See Jacques Derrida, " 'To Do Justice to Freud': The History of Madness in the Age of Psychoanalysis," trans. Pascale-Anne Brault and Michael Naas, in *Foucault and His Interlocutors*, ed. Arnold Davidson (Chicago: University of Chicago Press, 1997), pp. 85–86.

17. We could also call this "mortalism" a "machinism." The generation of incorruptibles is defined by a thought of life with the machine, but a kind of machine that contains the necessary possibility of breaking down, the necessary possibility of not going in the right direction, in short, a machine that is evil. This relation between life and machine will return in the conclusion. I have also used the word "life-ism" (in distinction from biologism or vitalism) to refer to this relation. See *The Implications of Immanence* (New York: Fordham University Press, 2006).

18. We cannot forget here Foucault's reflections on life and biopower.

19. In his dialogue with Roudinesco, Derrida provides a sort of bibliography of his writings on animals. See DQD 107 n. 2/210 n. 3. This "bibliography" has to some extent determined the selection of texts that I discuss here.

20. In *The Step Back*, David Wood has described a similar idea through the phrase "negative capability." See *The Step Back: Ethics and Politics after Deconstruction* (Albany: SUNY Press, 2005), pp. 6–7.

1. War and Scapegoats

1. See Hebrews 10:5–10.

2. In *Rogues*, Derrida says, "Hypothesis in Greek will have signified before all else the base, the infrastructure *posed* in what lies beneath a foundation. As such, it will have been a figure for the bottom [*fond*] or the basement, the groundwork or the foundation, and thus the principle of the thing, the reason of an institution, the rai-

son d'être of a science or a reasoning, of a logos or a logic, of a theory, rationalization, ratiocination. It will have also done this as the subject, substance, or supposition of a discourse, as a proposition, design, or resolution, but most often as a condition" (V 190/136). Sovereignty, in contrast, is unconditional and anhypothetical.

3. See the long discussion of the cold war that extends from CS11 142/92 to CS11 152/100.

4. Derrida does not cite any writing by John Paul II. But perhaps he had in mind the pope's 1993 encyclical, "Veritatas Splendor": "All around us we encounter contempt for human life after conception and before birth; the ongoing violation of basic rights of the person; the unjust destruction of goods minimally necessary for a human life. Indeed, something more serious has happened: man is no longer convinced that only in the truth can he find salvation. The saving power of the truth is contested, and freedom alone, uprooted from any objectivity, is left to decide by itself what is good and what is evil." See the Website of the United States Conference of Catholic Bishops: www.usccb.org/pope/writings.htm.

5. Michel Foucault, *Surveiller et punir* (Paris: Gallimard, 1975), p. 197; idem, *Discipline and Punish*, trans. Alan Sheridan (New York: Vintage, 1977), p. 168; Gilles Deleuze and Félix Guattari, *Capitalisme et schizophrénie 2: Mille plateaux* (Paris: Minuit, 1980), pp. 525 and 583; idem, *A Thousand Plateaus: Capitalism and Schizophrenia*, trans. Brian Massumi (Minneapolis: University of Minnesota Press, 1987), pp. 421 and 467.

6. Derrida's discussion of the return of the religious is simplified in the following outline:

SECOND SIGN: THE RETURN OF THE RELIGIOUS

Post-Kantian modernity saw a rise of secularization, but after the end of the cold war the religious returns. Two things about the return of the religious need to be explained.

A. *First (thing)*, the return of the religious is not a return, and it is not simple.

    1. The return is not a return because it is global and technological; this kind of being religious has never been seen before.

2. The return is not simple because
   a. On the one hand, fundamentalism (whether it is Islamic or Christian) is opposed to state or organized religions; this opposition implies a kind of destruction of religion.
   b. On the other hand, the return is a movement of peace (unify all Abrahamic religions); this movement of pacification is complicated since it involves the supreme values of human life (is this value higher than God?), and it involves a kind of religious colonization (or globalatinazation).
   c. Conclusion: the return is war by other means.
B. *Second (thing)*, the autoimmune nature of the return of the religious needs to be explained.
   1. The very thing fundamentalism opposes (technological progress) is used to oppose technological progress (example of 9/11).
   2. In other words, the poison is used by the "holy" to make the "holy."
   3. But also, besides technological violence, there is archaic violence, the violence of hands.
   4. Archaic violence is violence at the origin or at the root; this is structural violence.
   5. In general, in order to constitute the "holy" or the "unscathed," violence is necessary, which makes the "holy" violent and unholy.
   6. This autoimmune reaction, too, needs to be explained.

7. A fruitful comparison could be made between what Derrida says in *Rogues* and what Michael Hardt and Antonio Negri say in *Empire* (Cambridge: Harvard University Press, 2000) on the contemporary idea of "just war," which is justified not in terms of a transcendent principle but "justified in itself" (pp. 12–13).

8. See also "The University Without Condition," in *Without Alibi*, p. 224.

9. In order to think about this declosing in a more concrete way, one could look at the graffiti art being made on the Palestinian side of the wall that the Israelis are building between Israel (that is, between its settlements) and the West Bank. These artworks generally portray scenes that imply that one is looking through the wall, as if the wall is being dissolved or dismantled. These artworks, then, indicate the, in principle, divisibility (and destruction) of all wall-

like boundaries. For an interesting account of these artworks, see Cecilia Parsberg, "Networking on the wall," in the Internet journal *Eurozine* (www.eurozine.com), where one can also view some of the graffiti.

10. See also Serge Mergel, "Les dénominations orphiques de la survivance: Derrida et la question du pire," *L'animal autobiographique: Autour de Jacques Derrida*, ed. Marie-Louise Mallet (Paris: Galilée, 1999), pp. 441–468.

11. See Deleuze and Guattari, *Mille Plateaux*, p. 31; idem, *A Thousand Plateaus*, p. 21.

12. Immanuel Kant, *Religion Within the Bounds of Reason Alone*, trans. Theodore M. Greene and Hoyt H. Hudson (New York: Harper and Row, 1960), pp. 28, 32, and 38–39.

13. Foucault perhaps said it best: "thought is a certain mode of action where the other must become the same" (*Les mots et les choses* [Paris: Gallimard, 1966], p. 339; *The Order of Things*, trans. anonymous [New York: Vintage, 1970], p. 328).

14. Deleuze and Guattari, *Mille plateaux*, p. 281; idem, *A Thousand Plateaus*, p. 230.

15. Michel Foucault, *Histoire de la sexualité I: La volonté de savoir* (Paris: Gallimard, 1976), p. 179; idem, *The History of Sexuality: An Introduction*, trans. Robert Hurley (New York: Vintage, 1990), 1:136.

16. In "And Say the Animal Responded," Derrida questions the opposition between animalistic or, better, mechanical reaction and human responsibility: "Why do the stakes here seem to be so much higher? In problematizing, as I have done, the purity and the indivisibility of a line between reaction and response, and especially the possibility of tracing such a line, between the human in general and the animal in general, one risks—anxiety about such an idea and the subsequent objections to it cannot but be forthcoming— casting doubt on all responsibility, every ethics, every decision, and so on" (A 172–173/128).

17. Cf. Giorgio Agamben, *The Open: Man and Animal*, trans. Kevin Attell (Stanford, Calif.: Stanford University Press, 2004), p. 77: "The total humanization of the animal coincides with a total animalization of man."

18. Martin Heidegger, "The Self-assertion of the German University," trans. Karsten Harries, *Review of Metaphysics* 38, no. 151 (March

1985): 474–475; French translation found in *Ecrits politiques, 1933–1966* (Paris: Gallimard, 1995), p. 104.

19. In the English translation, "*voyou*" is rendered as "vagrant." My thanks to Michael Naas for alerting me to this usage.

20. Here Derrida wonders about the fact that Aristotle's *Politics* was not translated into Arabic during the Middle Ages, yet Plato's idea of the philosopher-king played a central role in Islamic "political philosophy."

21. Gilles Deleuze, "Renverser le platonisme," *Revue de métaphysique et de morale* 71, no. 4 (October–December 1966): 426–438; Michel Foucault, "Ceci n'est pas une pipe," in *Dits et écrits*, vol. 1, *1954–1975* (Paris: Gallimard, 2001), pp. 663–678 (English translation by James Harnes, as *This Is Not a Pipe* [Berkeley: University of California Press, 1983]).

"Renverser le platonisme" was later included in Gilles Deleuze, *Logique du sens* (Paris: Minuit, 1969), pp. 292–307 (English translation by Mark Lester with Charles Stivale, as *The Logic of Sense* [New York: Columbia University Press, 1990], pp. 253–266). The title of the original article in *Logique du sens* (and therefore also in the English translation) is incorrect. The title of the translation, in the appendix to *The Logic of Sense*, is "Plato and the Simulacrum." Deleuze also revised the article for its inclusion in *Logique du sens*. See Leonard Lawlor, *Thinking Through French Philosophy: The Being of the Question* (Bloomington: Indiana University Press, 2003), appendix 2, pp. 163–177, which contains an English translation of the original version of "Renverser le platonisme," by Heath Massey, who also annotated the translation. In Lawlor, see also chapter 8, "The Beginnings of Thought," pp. 123–141, for a comparison of Derrida and Deleuze. For more comparisons of Derrida and Deleuze, see Paul Patton and John Protevi, eds., *Deleuze and Derrida* (New York: Continuum, 2003).

22. On immanence in Derrida, see Jean-Luc Nancy, *Déconstruction du christianisme*, vol. 1, *La déclosion* (Paris: Galilée, 2005), p. 24 n. 1.

23. Martin Heidegger, *Nietzsche* (Pfullingen: Neske, 1961), 1:233; idem, *Nietzsche*, trans. David Farrell Krell (New York: Harper and Row, 1979), 1:201.

24. For more on deconstruction, see my "Derrida," in *The Stanford University Encyclopedia of Philosophy*, 2006, plato.stanford.edu.

25. Part 1 of "Plato's Pharmacy" (which is summarized at the beginning of part 2) concerns the characteristics of the pharmakon, while part 2 concerns the procedure of this metaphysical decision.

26. Martin Heidegger, *Wegmarken* (Frankfurt am Main, 1967), pp. 146–147; rev. ed. (Frankfurt am Main, 1976), pp. 312–313; idem, *Pathmarks*, trans. William McNeil (New York: Cambridge University Press, 1998), p. 240; my emphasis.

27. For more on "mixturism" in Merleau-Ponty in particular, see my *Implications of Immanence: Towards a New Concept of Life* (New York: Fordham University Press, 2006).

28. See also Gilles Deleuze, *Différence et répétition* (Paris: Presses Universitaires de France, 1968), p. 7; idem, *Difference and Repetition*, trans. Paul Patton (New York: Columbia University Press, 1994), p. 1: "Repetition is not generality."

29. What follows is a paraphrase of these pages from *De l'esprit*. "Origin heterogeneous" is to be understood at once, all at once, in four senses:

    1. Heterogeneous right off, from the origin, originally heterogeneous.
    2. Heterogeneous with respect to what is called the origin, other than the origin and irreducible to it.
    3. Heterogeneous and or insofar as at the origin, origin-heterogeneous because at the origin of the origin.
    4. Heterogeneous because (*parce que*) it is and although (*bien que*) it is at the origin. Because and although at the same time, it is this logical form of the tension that makes all this thinking hum (*vibrer*).

30. Here Derrida refers to the *Philebus*, 46a.

31. Here Derrida says,

    In a word, we do not believe that there exists, in all rigor, a Platonic text, closed in upon itself, complete with its inside and outside. Not that one must then consider that it is leaking on all sides and can be drowned confusedly in the undifferentiated generality of its element. Rather, provided the articulations are rigorously and prudently recognized, one should simply be able to untangle the hidden forces of attraction linking a present word with an absent word in the text of Plato. Some such force, given the *system* of the language, cannot *not* have acted upon the writing and reading of this text. With respect to the weight of such a force, the so-called "presence" of a quite relative verbal unit—the word—while not being a contingent accident worthy of no attention, nevertheless, does not constitute the ultimate criterion and the utmost pertinence.   (DIS 149/130; Derrida's emphasis)

32. See also Deleuze and Guattari, *Mille Plateaux*, p. 146; idem, *A Thousand Plateaus*, p. 116.

33. It is possible to determine four similarities (if not identities) between Heidegger's conception of life as the will to power in Nietzsche (in "Nietzsche's Word 'God is Dead'") and Foucault's conception of biopower (in *The History of Sexuality*, vol 1). First, both conceptions occur in the modern epoch, which is the epoch of anti-Platonism. Second, both conceptions, being modern, imply a transformation of vision into positing and constant presence. Third, biopower and will to power are commanding, meaning that the will in each conception superenhances the power that it already has; biowill to power is the will to more and more power (*super*abundant life). Finally, fourth, both Heidegger and Foucault associate the phenomenological concept of *Erlebnis* to biowill to power. I have argued for these identities in my *Implications of Immanence*, especially in chap. 10.

34. See, for example, the introduction to Hilary Kornbluth, ed., *Naturalizing Epistemology* (Cambridge, Mass.: MIT Press, 1987). Naturalizing has become so prevalent that in 2005 I received an essay to review for *Continental Philosophy Review* called "Naturalizing Deconstruction." Naturalizing deconstruction, however, is a ludicrous idea. In "What Is It Like to Be a Bat," *Mortal Questions* (New York: Cambridge University Press, 2006), Thomas Nagel questions the position of "physicalism" but does not advocate its rejection. In fact, he continues the project of "physicalism" when he opens up the possibility of an "objective phenomenology," which would describe subjective experience in objective, that is, in nonemotional and nonimaginary, terms. Such an objective phenomenology would not consider the singularity of a bat.

35. It is in this regard that Simon Glendinning misunderstands Derrida's criticisms of Heidegger on animality. Derrida's criticisms do not end up verifying the naturalistic outlook. See Simon Glendinning, "Heidegger and the Question of Animality," *International*

Journal of Philosophical Studies 4, no. 1 (1996): 67–86. See especially p. 83: "But freed from this [Cartesian] conception of animality we will not find it problematic to reject the idea that human life is separated from animal nature by an 'abyss.' For human life is itself a manifestation of nature—relatively distinctive no doubt, but not absolutely so. The conception does not ignore the difference between human beings and other animals, but it is *smoothly* naturalistic" (my emphasis). Derrida's examination of Heidegger's mode of differentiation between the world poverty of animals and the world-building ability of humans (which Glendinning has read and cites here) shows that Heidegger's own distinctions are anything but "smooth."

36. Foucault has used this term. See Michel Foucault, *La naissance de la clinique* (Paris: Presses Universitaires de France, 1997 [1963]), p. 148; idem, *The Birth of the Clinic*, trans. A. M. Sheridan Smith (New York: Vintage, 1994), p. 145. The English translation is based on the 1972 edition, which contains many changes from the original 1963 edition but also at times inserts passages from the original 1963 edition. The result is that the English translation is a confusing text. Concerning the revisions that Foucault made for the 1972 edition, see David Macey, *The Lives of Michel Foucault* (New York: Vintage, 1995), p. 133.

37. See Heidegger, *Wegmarken*, p. 296; rev. ed., p. 368; idem, *Pathmarks*, p. 228.

2. Animals Have No Hand

1. John Sallis has called this discourse "chorology." See John Sallis, *Chorology: On Beginning in Plato's Timaeus* (Bloomington: Indiana University Press, 1999), p. 96.

2. This sentence does not appear in the English translation on p. 121.

3. See *Politics*, 1253a9–10 and 1332b5; see also *De Anima*, 414b17.

4. Martin Heidegger, *Einführung in die Metaphysik* (Tübingen: Niemeyer, 1987 [1953]), pp. 50–51; idem, *Introduction to Metaphysics*, trans. Ralph Mannheim (New York: Doubleday, 1961), p. 66; Martin Heidegger, *Was Heißt Denken* (Tübingen, Niemeyer, 1961), pp. 174–175; idem, *What Is Called Thinking*, trans. J. Glenn Gray (New York: Harper and Row, 1968), p. 227; idem, *Qu'appelle-t-on penser,*

trans. Gérard Granel (Paris: Presses Universitaires de France, 1959), p. 261.

5. Martin Heidegger, *Was Heißt Denken*, p. 51; idem, *What Is Called Thinking*, p. 16; idem, *Qu'appelle-t-on penser*, p. 90.

6. I have insisted on using the correct title for this book instead of the title the English translation bears, *Speech and Phenomena*. See *Derrida and Husserl: The Basic Problem of Phenomenology* (Bloomington: Indiana University Press, 2002).

7. Martin Heidegger, *Die Grundbegriffe der Metaphysik, Welt— Endlichkeit—Einsamkeit* (Frankfurt am Main, 1983), p. 275; idem, *The Fundamental Problems of Metaphysics: World, Finitude, Solitude*, trans. William McNeil and Nicholas Walker (Bloomington: Indiana University Press, 1995), p. 186.

8. Cary Wolfe has also briefly examined these pages in Derrida. See Cary Wolfe, *Animal Rites: American Culture, the Discourse of Species, and Posthumanist Theory* (Chicago: University of Chicago Press, 2003), chap. 2, especially pp. 62–66.

9. Heidegger, *Was Heist Denken*, p. 51; idem, *What Is Called Thinking*, p. 16; idem, *Qu'appelle-t-on penser*, p. 90.

10. Derrida also thinks that Descartes, Kant, Levinas, and Lacan open up the same separation or limit between man and animal (see A 125–127).

11. Here Derrida cites Martin Heidegger, *Gesamtausgabe, Band 29/30, Die Grundbegriffe der Metaphysik, Welt—Endlichkeit—Einsamkeit* (Frankfurt am Main: Klostermann, 1983), p. 290. Derrida revised this passage for the essay's inclusion in *Psyché*, replacing the word "organ" with "animal." An English translation of the revised passage would look like this: "One could say also that the animal can only take or manipulate the thing insofar as it has nothing to do with the thing as such. It [the animal] does not let be what the thing is in its essence. It [the animal] has no access to the essence of the being as such."

12. See, for instance, David Wood, ed., *Of Derrida, Heidegger, and Spirit* (Evanston, Ill.: Northwestern University Press, 1993).

13. For other analyses of this distinction in Heidegger, see John Llewelyn, *The Middle Voice of Ecological Conscience* (New York: St. Martin's, 1991), pp. 155–156; also David Farrell Krell, *Daimon*

Life: Heidegger and Life-Philosophy (Bloomington: Indiana University Press, 1992), pp. 112–134.

14. I mentioned *steresis* in chapter 1 when I spoke of the *pharmakon* being that moment of nature that loves to hide.

15. See also Dennis Keenan's excellent reading of "Awaiting (at) the Arrival" in *The Question of Sacrifice* (Bloomington: Indiana University Press, 2005), pp. 140–146.

16. I shall return to the question of waiting in chapter 3. I can also now once again define a weak force: an inability to be unable to stop the event that is imminent from happening.

17. See Martin Heidegger, *Being and Time*, trans. John Macquarrie and Edward Robinson (New York: Harper and Row, 1962), p. 294.

18. Stambaugh's English translation also renders "steht bevor" as "stands before." See Martin Heidegger, *Being and Time*, trans. Joan Stambaugh (Albany: SUNY Press, 1996), p. 232.

19. Derrida's thought here is quite close to that of Levinas. See Emmanuel Levinas, *Autrement qu'être ou au-delà de l'essence* (The Hague: Martinus Nijhoff, 1974), p. 235; idem, *Otherwise than Being or Beyond Essence*, trans. Alphonso Lingis (The Hague: Martinus Nijhoff, 1981), p. 150.

20. For another discussion of Derrida's interpretation of this *"als,"* see François Raffoul, "Derrida et l'éthique de l'im-possible," forthcoming in a special issue of *Revue de métaphysique et de morale* on Derrida.

21. Derrida, of course, calls this difference "différance." It is here that we have the entire problem of repetition and memory.

22. See Michel Foucault, *Les mots et les choses* (Paris: Gallimard, 1966), p. 21; idem, *The Order of Things* (New York: Vintage, 1970), p. 5.

23. For more on spacing, see Jacques Derrida, *Le toucher: Jean-Luc Nancy* (Paris: Galilée, 2000).

24. But Merleau-Ponty's remarkable contribution to the human-animal relation must be acknowledged. See Ted Toadvine, " 'Strange Kinship': Merleau-Ponty on the Human-Animal Relation," in *Phenomenology of Life—From the Animal Soul to the Human Mind*, vol. 1, *In Search of Experience*, 17–32, Analecta Husserliana 93 (Dordrecht: Springer, 2006).

25. Democracy, majority rule, can be seen in the General Assembly,

while sovereignty is seen in supremacy of the permanent members of the Security Council and, chief among them, the two superpowers (V 143/100).

26. See Jacques Derrida, "La bête et le souverain," in *La démocratie à venir: Autour de Jacques Derrida* (Paris: Galilée, 2004): 433–476.

27. In addition, the mechanical character of the animal also means that animals cannot look at or gaze upon (*Blick, regard*) me (A 32/383). When animals look at me—Derrida speaks at length of Levinas's humanism in *L'animal que donc je suis*—they seem not to be the other who puts me in question; the gaze is reserved only for the "other man" (A 147). I shall turn to this problem of the gaze (blind eyes) in chapter 3.

28. Krell also stresses that Heidegger seems to reserve finitude only for humanity. See Krell, *Daimon Life*, p. 118.

29. See also Jacques Derrida, "Session of February 12, 1997," in "Hospitality," in *Acts of Religion*, ed. Gil Anidjar (London: Routledge, 2002), p. 384. Here Derrida says that, if I let someone die, "it means that I interpret it as a murder."

30. Jacques Derrida, "Et cetera . . . (and so on, und so weiter, and so forth, et ainsi de suite, und so überall, etc.)," in *Jacques Derrida*, ed. Marie-Louise Mallet and Ginette Michaud (Paris: Editions de l'Herne, 2004), p. 32; my emphasis; idem, *Deconstruction: A User's Guide*, ed. Nicolas Royle (London: Palgrave Macmillan, 2000), p. 300.

31. In "For the Love of Lacan," Derrida says, "In short, it would be a matter of contesting that death happens to some mortal being-for-death; rather, and this is a scandal for sense and for good sense, it happens only to some immortal who lacks for lacking nothing" (RPS 85/66).

32. Krell also stresses the literal sense of the term and its connection to misery. See Krell, *Daimon Life*, p. 118.

3. A More Sufficient Response?

1. The worst, which is the most suicidal, would allow us to open up, beyond the question of animality, the question of the environment, of global warming.

2. This dream perhaps alludes to Derrida's comment, quoted by David Wood, "I am a vegetarian in my soul." See David Wood, "Comment ne pas manger—Deconstruction and Humanism," in *Animal Others: On Ethics, Ontology, and Animal Life*, ed. H. Peter Steeves (Albany: SUNY Press, 1999), p. 20.

3. Michel Foucault, *Les mots et les choses* (Paris: Gallimard, 1966), p. 6; idem, *The Order of Things* (New York: Vintage, 1970), p. 22.

4. Jacques Lacan, *Ecrits* (Paris: Seuil, 1966), pp. 690, 692, 810; idem, *Ecrits: A Selection*, trans. Alan Sheridan (New York: Norton, 1977), pp. 285, 287, 308. Of course, early in "The Facteur of Truth," Derrida seemed to be criticizing Lacan. See PC 491–495/464–467. Derrida takes up this criticism again in RPS 78/59–60. It is important to note that Derrida stresses in "For the Love of Lacan" that his early reading of Lacan "did not claim to enclose or exhaust Lacan" (RPS 79/61). He goes on to say that he was not "criticizing" Lacan (RPS 81–82/63). If the symbolic in Lacan is based on the idea of a lack or privation, then we can see that what Derrida does with privation, that is, his attempt to make it positive, is in alliance with what Deleuze and Guattari did in *Anti-Oedipus* when they insisted on desire not being based in a lack, when they insist that desire is productive.

5. See chapter 6 of *La voix et le phénomène*.

6. The ambiguity of this term *"animalséance"* is complex. On the one hand, if we split the word as "ani-malséance," it means a kind of animated impropriety. On the other, if we split the word as "animal-séance," it means a session of the animal. Splitting the word this way makes it allude to Derrida's essay (found in *La dissemination*) called "La double séance" ("The Double Session").

7. Gilles Deleuze and Félix Guattari, *Capitalisme et schizophrénie 2. Mille plateaux* (Paris: Minuit, 1980), p. 375; idem, *A Thousand Plateaus: Capitalism and Schizophrenia*, trans. Brian Massumi (Minneapolis. University of Minnesota Press, 1987), p. 305. In his book on Francis Bacon, Deleuze identifies indiscernability with undecidability. See Gilles Deleuze, *Francis Bacon: Logique de la sensation* (Paris: Edition de la différence, 1981), p. 20; idem, *Francis Bacon: The Logic of Sensation*, trans. Daniel W. Smith (Minneapolis: University of Minnesota Press, 2003), p. 20. I have tried to show how close to-

gether yet distant from one another their thinking is: "for Deleuze, nonsense is immediately sense, and yet is divided from sense; for Derrida, nonsense is mediately sense and yet is united with sense" (Leonard Lawlor, *Thinking Through French Philosophy: The Being of the Question* [Bloomington: Indiana University Press, 2003], p. 132). These formulas maintain a very small difference between them. Indeed, Derrida would criticize Deleuze for being a "continuist" through the concept of immediacy (he made such a criticism in *Le toucher: Jean-Luc Nancy* [see TJLN 141–144/124–126], and Deleuze would criticize Derrida for being a "mediationist" through the concept of différance. But this small difference arises from a "point of diffraction": difference conceived as a relation that is defective, out of joint, unjust and unequal. As I have tried to show, this point of diffraction unifies what I am here calling "the generation of the incorruptibles." In the question of animality and life, we must, it seems to me, return to this point of diffraction and, by means of such a return, put the thought of Derrida and Deleuze into a relation of alliance. We must use all the resources of their respective forms of thinking in order to negotiate with the extreme positions of biological continuism and metaphysical separationism, in order, in other words, to find a more sufficient response to the worst.

8. See my *Imagination and Chance: The Difference Between the Thought of Ricœur and Derrida* (Albany: SUNY Press, 1992), pp. 17–24, which analyze Derrida's essay "White Mythology."

9. Cf. Deleuze and Guattari, *Capitalisme et schizophrénie 2*, pp. 286–287; idem, *A Thousand Plateaus*, pp. 234–235

10. Cf. Wood, "Comment ne pas manger," pp. 15–36.

11. On "mot d'ordre," see Deleuze and Guattari, *Capitalisme et schizophrénie 2*, p. 134; idem, *A Thousand Plateaus*, pp. 106–107.

12. Jacques Derrida, "Et cetera . . . (and so on, und so weiter, and so forth, et ainsi de suite, und so überall, etc.)," in *Jacques Derrida*, ed. Marie-Louise Mallet and Ginette Michaud (Paris: Editions de l'Herne, 2004), p. 32; idem, *Deconstructions: A User's Guide*, ed. Nicolas Royle (London: Palgrave Macmillan, 2000), p. 286. See also Deleuze and Guattari, *Capitalisme et schizophrénie 2*, p. 124; idem, *A Thousand Plateaus*, p. 98.

13. The inability has the same structure as the others like undeniability

or incorruptibility or unforgivability. Animals are able (actively) to take up the inability, which means that they are able to allow themselves not to respond. This inability necessarily means that they can also respond in countless ways, all of which would be insufficient in relation to the proper meaning of responding (if we were able to determine a proper meaning of the verb "to respond").

14. See Gilles Deleuze, *Logique du sens* (Paris: Minuit, 1969), pp. 10–11; idem, *The Logic of Sense*, trans. Mark Lester with Charles Stivale (New York: Columbia University Press, 1990), pp. 2–3.

15. Martin Heidegger, *Unterwegs zur Sprache* (Pfullingen: Neske, 1982), p. 175; idem, *On the Way to Language*, trans. Peter D. Hertz (New York: Harper and Row, 1971), p. 71; idem, *Acheminement vers la parole*, trans. Jean Beaufret, Wolfgang Brokmeier, and François Fédier (Paris: Gallimard, 1976), p. 159. The French translation is: "Qu'apprenons-nous quand nous pensons et repensons assez cela? Que ce n'est pas questionner qui est le propre geste de la pensée, mais: prêter l'oreille à la parole où se promet ce qui devra venir en la question."

16. See Heidegger, *Acheminement vers la parole*, p. 164 n. 4. My translation.

17. The citation can be found in Martin Heidegger, *Holzwege* (Frankfurt am Main: Klostermann, 2003), p. 343; English translation by David Farrell Krell and Frank A. Capuzzi in Martin Heidegger, *Early Greek Thinking* (New York: Harper and Row, 1975), p. 57. Heidegger also rejects scientific proof here.

18. For a fuller examination of the promise, see my *Derrida and Husserl: The Basic Problem of Phenomenology* (Bloomington: Indiana University Press, 2002), pp. 216–225.

19. The silence of animals is precisely the topic selected by Elizabeth de Fontenay in her exhaustive historical study of the role of animality in Western philosophy. See Elizabeth de Fontenay, *Le silence des bêtes* (Paris: Fayard, 1998).

20. Jacques Derrida, "Circonfession," in Geoffrey Bennington and Jacques Derrida, *Jacques Derrida* (Paris: Seuil, 1991), p. 62; idem, "Circumfession," in Geoffrey Bennington and Jacques Derrida, *Jacques Derrida*, trans. Geoffrey Bennington (Chicago: The University of Chicago Press, 1993), p. 62.

21. In this regard, we need to recall, then, what Paul wrote to the Romans (VIII:19): "For the creation [and the creatures] wait with eager longing for the revelation." Heidegger recalls this passage in the discussion of the essence of animality. See Martin Heidegger, *Gesamtausgabe, Band 29/30, Die Grundbegriffe der Metaphysik: Welt—Endlichkeit—Einsamkeit* (Frankfurt am Main: Klostermann, 1983), p. 396; idem, *The Fundamental Concepts of Metaphysics: World, Finitude, Solitude*, trans. William McNeill and Nicholas Walker (Bloomington: Indiana University Press, 1995), p. 273. See also chapter 4 of my *Implications of Immanence: Toward a New Concept of Life* (New York: Fordham University Press, 2006).

22. In "For the Love of Lacan," Derrida says, "The remarkable things Lacan says on the animal are also in my view most problematic" (RPS 85/66).

23. See Lacan, *Ecrits*, p. 807; idem, *Ecrits: A Selection*, p. 305.

24. See also Deleuze and Guattari, *Capitalisme et schizophrénie 2*, p. 145; idem, *A Thousand Plateaus*, p. 115.

25. Gilles Deleuze, "A quoi reconnaît-on le structuralisme?" in *L'île déserte et autres textes* (Paris: Minuit, 2002), pp. 238–269; idem, "How Do We Recognize Structuralism?" trans. Melissa McMahon, in *Desert Islands and Other Texts* (New York: Semiotext(e), 2004), pp. 170–192.

26. In regard to Deleuze's understanding of structuralism, one should examine Derrida's second essay on Levinas ("At This Very Moment"), which entirely concerns seriality.

27. See also Deleuze and Guattari, *Capitalisme et schizophrénie 2*, pp. 289–290; idem, *A Thousand Plateaus*, pp. 236–237.

28. Deleuze, "A quoi reconnaît-on le structuralisme?" p. 266; idem, "How Do We Recognize Structuralism?" p. 190. See also Jacques Lacan, *Les quatres concepts fondamentaux de la psychanalyse* (Paris: Seuil, Essais, 1973), p. 88; idem, *The Four Fundamental Concepts of Psycho-analysis*, trans. Alan Sheridan (New York: Norton, 1978), p. 75. Here, Lacan says, "The subject [in the dream] does not see where it [*ça*: the id] is going, he follows [*suit*]." "Suit," as we know from Derrida, is a homonym with "suis," as in "Je suis," the first person singular of the French verb "*être*," "to be," which implies that what is issue here is the question of being, the being of the "cogito."

29. For more on "originary finitude," see Edmund Husserl, *L'origine de la géométrie*, trans. and intro. Jacques Derrida (Paris: Presses Universitaires de France, 1974 [1962]), p. 108; idem, *Edmund Husserl's Origin of Geometry: An Introduction*, trans. John P. Leavey (Lincoln: University of Nebraska Press, 1989 [1978]), p. 105. See also Michel Foucault, *La naissance de la clinique* (Paris: Presses Universitaires de France, 1997 [1963]), p. 201; idem, *The Birth of the Clinic*, trans. A. M. Sheridan Smith (New York: Vintage, 1994), p. 197. For a more contemporary use of the phrase "finitude originaire," see Françoise Dastur, *Phénoménologie en questions* (Paris: Vrin, 2004), p. 104.

30. It also concerns Derrida's relation to Gadamer and to hermeneutics. See also Gadamer's excellent reading of Celan in Hans-Georg Gadamer, *Gadamer on Celan*, trans. and ed. Richard Heinemann and Bruce Krajewski (Albany: SUNY Press, 1997). For another reading of *Béliers*, see Marc Crépon, "C'est l'éthique même," in *Langues sans demeure* (Paris: Galilée, 2005), pp. 67–85.

31. See Paul Celan, *Poems of Paul Celan: Revised and Expanded*, trans. Michael Hamburger (New York: Persea, 2002), pp. 250–251. Here is the entire poem:

GROSSE, GLÜHENDE WÖLBUNG

mit dem sich
hinaus- und hinweg-
wühlenden Schwarzgestirn-
    Schwarm:

der verkieselten Stirn eines Widders
brenn ich dies Bild ein, zwischen
die Hörner, darin,
im Gesang der Windungen, das
Mark der geronnenen
Herzmeere schwillt.
Wo-
gegen
rennt er nicht an?

Die Welt ist fort, ich muß dich
        tragen.

Vast, Glowing Vault

with the swarm of
black stars pushing them-
selves out and away:

onto a ram's silicified forehead
I brand this image, between
the horns, in which,
in the song of the whorls, the
marrow of melted
heart-oceans swells.
In-
to what
does he not charge?

The world is gone, I must carry you.

32. In *Rogues*, Derrida says,

Where the so-called globalization [*mondialization*] is more in-egalitarian and violent than ever, therefore, more alleged and less worldwide
than ever, where there is no *the* world, and where we, we who are without world [*sans monde*], *weltlos, form* a world only against a backdrop
[*fond*] of a non-world where there is neither world nor even that poor-
in-world that Heidegger attributes to the animal (which would be, according to him, *weltarm*). Within this abyss of the without-world [*sans-
monde*], this abyss without support, indeed on the condition of this
absence of support, bottom, ground, or foundation, it is as if one *bore*
[*portait*] the other, as if I felt, without support and without hypothesis,
borne [*porté*] by the other, and borne [*porté*] toward the other, as if, as
Celan says, *Die Welt ist fort, ich muss dich tragen*: the world goes away;
the world disappears; I must bear you, where the world would no longer

or would not yet be, where the world would distance itself, get lost in the distance, or be still to come.   (V 213/155)

33. See also Jacques Derrida, "Session of January 8, 1997," in "Hospitality," in *Acts of Religion*, ed. Gil Anidjar (London: Routledge, 2002), p. 359.

34. Here, we would have to take up the complicated and extraordinary work done by Tom Regan in *The Case for Animal Rights* (Berkeley: University of California Press, 1985). It seems to me that, in general, Regan wants to extend something like personhood, which would grant the status of requiring ethical consideration, to certain kinds of animals (mammalians). The status of person, however, reproduces the exclusionary structure of the self that is precisely in question here, following Derrida. Instead, the strategy here is to deprive man of personhood, which results in a kind of equality between man and animals. Then we have no right (rights have been taken from us) to treat the animals as radically different from ourselves. Nevertheless, the staggered analogy idea implies a kind of extension of human subjectivity to animals, putting our position into proximity with that of Regan, and the emphasis on the proper name reinforces this proximity. The proper name, however, is always insufficient.

35. For Derrida, even though this kind of subjectivity is "post," it really remains Cartesian. The demonstration of this Cartesian legacy is the main idea in *L'animal que donc je suis*.

36. Derrida continues, "Deconstruction therefore calls for a different kind of rights, or, rather, lets itself be called by a more exacting articulation of rights, prescribing, in a different way, more responsibility" (PS 288/273).

37. It is impossible to deny that what Derrida is doing with replacement resembles what Levinas is doing with substitution. Yet, in *Otherwise than Being*, Levinas associates substitution with "human fraternity." See Emmanuel Levinas, *Autrement qu'être ou au-delà de l'essence* (The Hague: Martinus Nijhoff, 1974), p. 184; idem, *Otherwise than Being or Beyond Essence*, trans. Alphonso Lingis (The Hague: Martinus Nijhoff, 1981), p. 116. See also "The Paradox of Morality: An Interview with Emmanuel Levinas," in *The Provoca-*

tion of Levinas, ed. Robert Bernasconi and David Wood (London: Routledge, 1988), p. 169. where Levinas says, "Yet the priority of here is not found in the animal, but in the human face. We understand the animal, the face of an animal, in accordance with Dasein. The phenomenon of the face is not in its purest form in the dog." See also p. 172, where Levinas says, "This is my principal thesis. A being is something that is attached to being, to its own being. This is Darwin's idea. The being of animals is a struggle for life." Levinas then goes on to say man can also be saintly, which is being more attached to the being of the other than to his own. The question, however, is: is it not possible for an animal to be saintly? Anecdotally, one can think of animals being devoted to their offspring and to their mates. But we can wonder about man as not being saintly. If man is also able not to be saintly, to be animalistic, if he has this unactualized possibility, then is it not possible that animals have this unactualized possibility? See also Silvia Benso's excellent account of the nature of alterity in Levinas: Silvia Benso, *The Face of Things: A Different Side of Ethics* (Albany: SUNY Press, 2000), pp. 42–44.

38. See also Derrida, "Session of January 8, 1997," p. 363.

39. Jacques Derrida, "Session of May 7, 1997," in "Hospitality," pp. 419–420.

40. See Levinas, *Autrement qu'être ou au-delà de l'essence*, pp. 190, 205; idem, *Otherwise than Being or Beyond Essence*, pp. 120, 129.

41. Dennis Keenan provides an excellent account of sacrifice in Derrida in his *Question of Sacrifice* (Bloomington: Indiana University Press, 2005), see pp. 136–137, especially. See also de Fontenay, *Le silence des bêtes*, p. 714. The use of this phrase "sacrifice sacrifice" indicates that we cannot avoid all violence; we are seeking the least violence, and the least violence could still be characterized as sacrifice.

42. Perhaps this openness to all others whatsoever is compatible with Haraway's discourse on cyborgs and companion species. See Donna Haraway, "Cyborgs to Companion Species: Reconfiguring Kinship in Technoscience," in *The Haraway Reader* (London: Routledge, 2004), pp. 295–320.

43. It is possible that the structure I am about to describe is inspired by Islam since Derrida at this point in "A Word of Welcome" cites

Louis Massignon's study *L'hospitalité sacrée* (Paris: Nouvelle Cité, 1987). See also Derrida, "Hospitality," pp. 365–402.

44. Here, I could add another comment from Deleuze and Guattari: "Never believe that a smooth space will suffice to save us [*ne jamais croire qu'un espace lisse suffit à nous sauver*]" (*Capitalisme et schizophrénie 2*, p. 500; idem, *A Thousand Plateaus*, p. 625).

45. Deleuze and Guattari, *Capitalisme et schizophrénie 2*, p. 186; idem, *A Thousand Plateaus*, p. 150.

46. Celan speaks of this date. Lenz is a character in Georg Büchner's novella *Lenz*. See *Büchner: The Complete Plays*, ed. Michael Patterson (London: Metheun, 2002), pp. 249–277. Celan spoke of this date in his address "Meridian"; see Jacques Derrida, *Sovereignties in Question: The Poetics of Paul Celan* (New York: Fordham University Press, 2005), p. 180. I should also note that Deleuze and Guattari open *Anti-Oedipus* with a discussion of Lenz's walk in the mountains. See Gilles Deleuze and Felix Guattari, *Capitalisme et schizophrénie: L'anti-œdipe* (Paris: Minuit, 1972/1973), p. 7; idem, *Anti-Oedipus: Capitalism and Schizophrenia*, trans. Robert Hurley, Mark Seem, and Helen R. Lane (New York: Viking, 1977), p. 2.

47. For more on the date in Deleuze and Derrida, see Jay Lampert, *Deleuze and Guattari's Philosophy of History* (London: Continuum, 2006), pp. 84–87. While I recognize Lampert's attempt in these pages to make sense of this intersection between Derrida and Deleuze, I am not convinced by the arguments. Most important, both try to make loss something positive.

48. "*Bestand*" is the word, of course, that Heidegger uses to designate the mode of presencing in modern technology; see Martin Heidegger, "The Question Concerning Technology," in *The Question Concerning Technology and Other Essays*, trans. J. Glenn Gray (New York: Harper, 1977), p. 17.

49. Cary Wolfe has also commented on this idea in Derrida. See Cary Wolfe, *Animal Rites: American Culture, the Discourse of Species, and Posthumanist Theory* (Chicago: University of Chicago Press, 2003), pp. 107–109. Wolfe takes a related but different approach from the one I am advocating here. He tries to show that animals (in the plural) are worthy of being in a "moral community" even if they cannot reciprocate moral consideration, that is, be the "addressee"

of a moral "call." On the one hand, I am not posing the problem in these "Levinasian" ethical terms. Instead, I am starting from a problem (the problem of the worst) and then seeking a solution, albeit insufficient. On the other hand, like Wolfe, I am trying to find a way to make animals, all of them, be worthy of being members of a moral community. But this membership is based on a different idea. I am trying to find a way to make us (those of us who want to sacrifice) restrain ourselves in relation to them (indeed, in relation to the whole earth: this is an excessive demand), and this would be done by the demand that all of them without exception be named.

50. Jacques Derrida, "Comment nommer," in *Le poète que je cherche à être: Cahier de Michel Deguy*, ed. Yves Charnet (Paris: La Table Ronde, 1996), p. 184: "Saluer, ce n'est pas seulement nommer, c'est appeler l'autre comme il s'appelle ou comme elle s'appelle."

51. As Deleuze would say, the proper name must be separated from its traditional link to the general noun. In other words, one must lose one's proper name in order to be named properly. See Deleuze, *Logique du sens*, p. 11; idem, *The Logic of Sense*, p. 3. See also Marc Crépon, *Langues sans demeure*, p. 61: "By dreaming, right on language, the invention of an idiom that resists all translation, I dream therefore of a language that would know how to support [*donner droit*] all of what comes—a language that, far from appropriating to itself beings and things, would offer to them this supreme form of attention, which consists in saying, in a unique language, their singularity" (my translation).

52. See Deleuze and Guattari, *Capitalisme et schizophrénie 2*, pp. 323–324; idem, *A Thousand Plateaus*, pp. 263–265. There, speaking of haecceity, Deleuze and Guattari say, "This semiotic is composed above all of proper names, verbs in the infinitive and indefinite articles or pronouns."

53. A long examination of Derrida's relation to Levinas could begin here. Minimally, we would have to quote this passage from *Otherwise than Being* in the "Substitution" chapter: "To communicate is indeed to open oneself, but the openness is not complete if it is in the watch for recognition. It is complete not in the opening to the spectacle or of the recognition to for the other, but in becoming a

responsibility for him. The 'emphase' of openness is responsibility for the other to the point of substitution, where the for-the-other that is proper to disclosure and to monstration to the other, turning into [*virant en*] the for-the-other that is proper to responsibility. This is the thesis of the present work" (Levinas, *Autrement qu'être ou au-delà de l'essence*, p. 189; idem, *Otherwise than Being or Beyond Essence*, p. 119). But, as the conclusion demonstrates, what defines Derrida's thought is the idea of a certain machinic or technological repetition being irreducible. One can find this machinic repetition in Deleuze and Foucault; it defines the generation of the incorruptibles. For Derrida, the machinic repetition (in a word, writing) determines contamination and the same. This kind of sameness, it seems to me, is alien to Levinas's thought and therefore keeps him separate from the generation of the incorruptibles. Cf. Derrida, "Session of March 5, 1997," in "Hospitality," p. 409: "Therefore, substitution and cloning, series and irreplaceability: is a clone identical or different only *solo numero* (homozygotic twin). Without entering into the scientific debate (contestation as to the novelty, the consequences, etc.). Ask whether this changes anything for ethics of substitution (Levinas-Massignon), birth and death, letting be born, letting die."

54. If you take the idea seriously that all experience and thought works on the basis of a medium of sameness, then "vegetarianism" (the attempt not to internalize or "eat" animals) is impossible or necessarily entangled with "carnivorism" (The internalization done to all things). It is necessary to internalize, "eat," do violence to—just in order to think about something other like an animal or a vegetable. Using a homonymic association, we could say that vegetarianism "e(s)t" carnivorism, which would mean not only that the two practices are conjoined and therefore different from one another but also that one is the same as the other. The idea of a medium of sameness does not allow for such a position of pure vegetarianism. The position ends up being naive, given the structural or essential necessity of internalization. I am a practicing vegetarian, but at holidays I eat meat. Cf. what Elizabeth de Fontanay says in her interview, p. 6: "Le vivant et l'animal, entretien avec Elizabeth de Fontenay," online at www.philagora.net/philo-fac/le-vivant/

vivant-animal6.htm. For asceticism, see Deleuze and Guattari, *Capitalisme et schizophrénie 2*, p. 342; *A Thousand Plateaus*, p. 279.

55. Derrida, "Session of January 8, 1997," p. 372.

56. This "step back" alludes to David Wood's work *The Step Back: Ethics and Politics after Deconstruction* (Albany: SUNY Press, 2005). Wood's book opens with an epigram from Heidegger speaking of the "step back," which alludes to *Gelassenheit*. On my photocopy version of "Il faut bien manger," which comes from its original publication in *Confrontation* (1989), there is an inscription from Derrida, which says, "vers [toward] 'a generalized *Gelassenheit*' which lets be . . . animals (and whatever)."

57. The role of "radical evil" here should make one hesitate before one associates what Derrida says or what I am saying with liberalism. If peace (with peace), that is, nonviolence, defines the aim of liberalism, then we cannot categorize the slogan "violence against violence" as a liberal slogan. On liberalism and nonviolence, see Maurice Merleau-Ponty, *Humanisme et terreur* (Paris: Idées/Gallimard, 1980 [1947]), especially, p. 47; idem, *Humanism and Terror*, trans. John O'Neill (Boston: Beacon, 1969), especially, p. xx. The aim of nonviolence in liberalism is synonymous with the desire to have a good conscience, to think that, by being a vegetarian, for example, one can stop worrying about animal welfare and sleep well at night. The main idea for me, however, is that evil and violence, radical evil, cannot be reduced, cannot be eliminated from the roots of life itself, and therefore there is no escape from bad conscience. Here we can add that all "lifeism" is based in "mortalism." For more on lifeism and mortalism, see Lawlor, *The Implications of Immanence*, especially chap. 10. If one of our slogans is "violence against violence," then we must affirm that violence may be necessary in order to institute something like unconditional hospitality.

58. For more on forgiveness in Derrida and an entire theory of forgiveness, see Kelly Oliver, *The Colonization of Psychic Space: A Psychoanalytic Social Theory of Oppression* (Minneapolis: University of Minnesota Press, 2004), pp. 179–200.

59. See Clément Rosset, *Logique du pire: Elément pour une philosophie tragique* (Paris: Presses Universitaires de France, 1971). Inspired by

Deleuze's *Logique du sens*, this remarkable book, as the subtitle indicates, concerns "tragic philosophy." Rosset says,

> Even therefore if the tragic thinker took into philosophical consideration ideologies that he judged to be absurd, he would engage in no battle against them, since he has no ideology to propose in their stead or in place of them. Making use of "nothing" upon which to ground himself in order to push opinions and beliefs away, he will tolerate them, necessarily all of them. Tragic philosophy makes use then of a virtue that is inseparable from the "moral" order: a capacity of tolerance to every experience, which in this way it can claim as its own good (all nonunconditional tolerance being, in its eyes, intolerance).
>
> (p. 154; my translation)

It is unfortunate that no English translation of this book exists. Nevertheless, what Rosset says here seems to resonate with Derrida's comments about tolerance in "Faith and Knowledge" about a "new tolerance" (see FS 32–34/21–22, paragraphs 25–26).

60. See "Convention on the Rights of the Child, G.A. res. 44/25, annex, 44 U.N. GAOR Supp. (No. 49) at 167, U.N. Doc. A/44/49 (1989), *entered into force* Sept. 2 1990." This text can be found online at www1.umn.edu/humanrts/instree/k2crc.htm. Article 7, clause 1, states, "The child shall be registered immediately after birth and shall have the right from birth to a name, the right to acquire a nationality and, as far as possible, the right to know and be cared for by his or her parents." This article provides support for the importance or necessity of the name. But it is not my intention to suggest that animals have a right to a name. Because every singularity is necessarily connected to iterability, naming cannot be avoided. What I am advocating, on the basis of the fact of singularity, is a certain kind of naming, a naming well, that reduces violence against animals and guards their singularity for the future.

61. In order to pay off, the bet, however, requires a transformative experience, a conversion experience, an experience, as Deleuze would say, of the "sentiendum."

62. There is an "unlivable contradiction" here in the concept of hospitality: unconditional and conditional at the same time. See Derrida, "Hospitality: Session of January 8, 1997," p. 360. Or, see Jacques Derrida, "Une certain possibilité impossible de dire l'événement," in *Dire l'événement, est-ce possible?* (Paris: L'Harmattan, 2001), p. 98. Here, Derrida says that the event appears as such only as being repeatable; uniqueness as such is thinkable only as iterable. Substitution replaces the irreplaceable.

63. See also Deleuze and Guattari, *Capitalisme et schizophrénie 2*, p. 294; idem, *A Thousand Plateaus*, p. 240. Here, Deleuze and Guattari speak of being "responsible in principle before" animals because of the affectivity of animals. In *Francis Bacon*, Deleuze (without Guattari) is even more insistent on responsibility "before" (*devant*) the animals. See Deleuze, *Francis Bacon: Logique de la sensation*, p. 21; *Francis Bacon: The Logic of Sensation*, p. 22.

64. Here, we could open the question, what is a suicide bomber? Noah Feldman, in an article in the *New York Times*, has shown that the reasoning that supports suicide bombers could be extended to the use of nuclear weapons, a use that would be completely suicidal. In short, without saying this, Feldman describes what Derrida has called the logic of autoimmunity, the worst. See Noah Feldman, "Islam, Terror and the Second Nuclear Age," *New York Times Magazine*, October 29, 2006, pp. 50–57, 72, and 76–79, especially p. 56.

65. See Giorgio Agamben, *The Time That Remains*, trans. Patricia Dailey (Stanford, Calif.: Stanford University Press, 2005), pp. 96–97.

66. For a new concept of vocality, see Fred Evans, *The Multi-Voiced Body: Society, Communication, and the Age of Diversity* (New York: Columbia University Press, forthcoming).

67. Jean-Luc Nancy, "La déconstruction du christianisme," in *Déconstruction du christianisme*, vol. 1, *La déclosion* (Paris: Galilée, 2005), p. 208; idem, "The Deconstruction of Christianity," trans. Simon Sparks, in *Religion and Media*, ed. Hent de Vries and Samuel Weber (Stanford, Calif.: Stanford University Press, 2001), p. 116.

68. Nancy calls the belief that the origin of Christianity is unified "projection de Noël" (Christmas projection), in "La déconstruction du christianisme," p. 211; "The Deconstruction of Christianity," p. 118.

69. "*Ça*" is the French translation of Freud's "*Es*," the id, as we say in English. "*Ça*" is also a homonym with "*sa*," which is an abbreviation Derrida has made for "le savoir absolu" in Hegel in *Glas*.

Conclusion

1. Gille Deleuze and Félix Guattari, *Capitalisme et schizophrénie 2: Mille Plateaux* (Paris: Minuit, 1980), p. 130; idem, *A Thousand Plateaus: Capitalism and Schizophrenia*, trans. Brian Massumi (Minneapolis: University of Minnesota Press, 1987), p. 103.

2. On this point, compare what Deleuze and Guattari say: "To be bilingual, multilingual, but in one and the same language, without even a dialect or a patois. To be a bastard, a half-breed, but through a purification of race" (*Mille Plateaux*, p. 125; *A Thousand Plateaus*, p. 98).

BIBLIOGRAPHY

Texts by Jacques Derrida

Books

Adieu à Emmanuel Levinas. Paris: Galilée, 1997. English translation by Michael Naas and Pascale-Anne Brault, as *Adieu to Emmanuel Levinas*. Stanford, Calif.: Stanford University Press, 1999.

L'animal que donc je suis. Paris: Galilée, 2006. English translation of chapter 1 by David Wills, as "The Animal that Therefore I Am (More to Follow)," in *Critical Inquiry* 28 (Winter 2002): 369–418. English translation of chapter 3 by David Wills, as "And Say the Animal Responded," in *Zoontologies: The Question of the Animal*, ed. Cary Wolfe, 121–146. Minneapolis: University of Minnesota Press, 2003.

Anne Dufourmantelle invite Jacques Derrida à répondre: De l'hospitalité. Paris: Calmann-Lévy, 1997. English translation by Rachel Bowlby, as *Of Hospitality: Anne Dufourmantelle Invites Jacques Derrida to Respond*. Stanford, Calif.: Stanford University Press, 2000.

Apories. Paris: Galilée, 1996. English translation by Thomas Dutoit, as *Aporias*. Stanford, Calif.: Stanford University Press, 1993.

L'archéologie du frivole: Lire Condillac. Paris: Denoël/Gontheier, 1973. English translation by John P. Leavey, Jr., as *The Archeology of the Frivolous: Reading Condillac*. Pittsburgh: Duquesne University Press, 1980.

Béliers. Paris: Galilée, 2003. English translation by Thomas Dutoit and Phillippe Romanski, as "Rams," in *Sovereignties in Question: The Poetics of Paul Celan*, 135–163. New York: Fordham University Press, 2005.

La carte postale de Socrate à Freud et au-delà. Paris: Flammarion, 1980. English translation by Alan Bass, as *The Postcard from Socrates to Freud and Beyond*. Chicago: University of Chicago Press, 1987.

Chaque fois unique, la fin du monde. Paris: Galilée, 2003. Originally published in English as *The Work of Mourning*. Ed. Pascale-Anne Brault and Michael Naas. Chicago: University of Chicago Press, 2001.

Le "concept" du 11 septembre: Dialogues à New York (octobre–décembre 2001) avec Giovanna Borradori. With Jürgen Habermas. Paris: Galilée, 2004. Originally published in English as *Philosophy in the Time of Terror: Dialogues with Jürgen Habermas and Jacques Derrida*. Chicago: University of Chicago Press, 2003.

De l'esprit. Paris: Galilée, 1987. English translation by Geoff Bennington and Rachel Bowlby, as *Of Spirit*. Chicago: University of Chicago Press, 1989.

De la grammatologie. Paris: Minuit, 1967. English translation by Gayatri Spivak, as *Of Grammatology*. Baltimore: Johns Hopkins University Press, 1974.

De quoi demain . . . Dialogue. Paris: Fayard/Galilée, 2001. English translation by Jeff Fort, as *For What Tomorrow . . . A Dialogue*. Stanford, Calif.: Stanford University Press, 2004.

Demeure. Paris: Galilée, 1998. English translation by Elizabeth Rottenberg, as "Demeure: Fiction and Testimony," in Maurice Blanchot, *The Instant of My Death*, 13–102. Stanford, Calif.: Stanford University Press, 2000.

Dire l'événement, est-ce possible? Paris: L'Harmattan, 2001.

La dissemination. Paris: Seuil, 1972. English translation by Barbara Johnson, as *Dissemination*. Chicago: University of Chicago Press, 1981.

Donner le temps: 1. La fausse monnaie. Paris: Galilée, 1991. English translation by Peggy Kamuf, as *Given Time: 1. Counterfeit Money*. Chicago: University of Chicago Press, 1992.

Du droit à la philosophie. Paris: Galilée, 1990. Partial English translation by Jan Plug and others, as *Eyes of the University: Right to Philosophy 2*. Stanford, Calif.: Stanford University Press, 2004.

L'écriture et la différence. Paris: Seuil, 1967. English translation by Alan Bass, as *Writing and Difference.* Chicago: University of Chicago Press, 1978.

Etats d'âme de la psychanalyse. Paris: Galilée, 2000. English translation in *Without Alibi,* listed below.

Force de loi. Paris: Galilée, 1994. English translation by Mary Quaintance, as "Force of Law: The Mystical Foundation of Authority," in *Deconstruction and the Possibility of Justice,* ed. Drucilla Cornell, Michael Rosenfeld, and David Gray Carlson, 3–67. New York: Routledge, 1992.

Glas. 2 vols. Paris: Denoël/Gontheier, 1981 [1974]. English translation by John P. Leavey, Jr., and Richard Rand, as *Glas.* Lincoln: University of Nebraska Press, 1986.

Husserl, Edmund. *L'origine de la géométrie.* Trans. and intro. Jacques Derrida. Paris: Presses Universitaires de France, 1974 [1962]. English translation by John P. Leavey, as *Edmund Husserl's Origin of Geometry: An Introduction.* Lincoln: University of Nebraska Press, 1989 [1978].

Khôra. Paris: Galilée, 1993. English translation by Ian McLeod, as "Khōra," in *On the Name,* ed. Thomas Dutoit, 89–127. Stanford, Calif.: Stanford University Press, 1995.

Limited Inc. Paris: Galilée, 1990. Originally published in English as *Limited Inc,* trans. Samuel Weber. Reprint, Evanston, Ill.: Northwestern University Press, 1988 [1974].

Marges de la philosophie. Paris: Minuit, 1972. English translation by Alan Bass, as *Margins of Philosophy.* Chicago: University of Chicago Press, 1982.

Mémoires d'aveugle: L'autoportrait et autres ruines. Paris: Editions de la Réunion des musées nationaux, 1990. English translation by Pascale-Anne Brault and Michael Naas, as *Memories of the Blind: The Self-Portrait and Other Ruins.* Chicago: University of Chicago Press, 1993.

Mémoires pour Paul de Man. Paris: Galilée, 1988. Originally published in English as *Memoires for Paul de Man.* Trans. Cecile Lindsay, Jonathan Culler, and Eduardo Cadava. New York: Columbia University Press, 1986.

Le monolinguisme de l'autre. Paris: Galilée, 1996. English translation by Patrick Mensah, as *Monolingualism of the Other*. Stanford, Calif.: Stanford University Press, 1998.

L'oreille de l'autre: Otobiographies, transferts, traductions. Textes et débats avec Jacques Derrida. Montreal: VLB, 1982. English translation by Peggy Kamuf, as *The Ear of the Other: Otobiography, Transference, Translation. Texts and Discussions with Jacques Derrida*. New York: Schocken, 1985.

Points de suspension: Entretiens. Paris: Galilée, 1992. English translation by Peggy Kamuf and others, as *Points . . . Interviews, 1974–1994*, ed. Elizabeth Weber. Stanford, Calif.: Stanford University Press, 1995.

Politiques de l'amitié. Paris: Galilée, 1994. English translation by George Collins, as *Politics of Friendship*. London: Verso, 1997.

Positions. Paris: Minuit, 1972. English translation by Alan Bass, as *Positions*. Chicago: University of Chicago Press, 1981.

Le problème de la genèse dans la philosophie de Husserl. Paris: Presses Universitaires de France, 1990. English translation by Marion Hobson, as *The Problem of Genesis in Husserl's Philosophy*. Chicago: University of Chicago Press, 2003.

Psyche: Inventions de l'autre. Paris: Galilée, 1987.

Psyche: Inventions de l'autre, II. Paris: Galilée, 2003.

Résistances de la psychanalyse. Paris: Galilée, 1996. English translation by Peggy Kamuf, Pascale-Anne Brault, and Michael Naas, as *Resistances of Psychoanalysis*. Stanford, Calif.: Stanford University Press, 1998.

Sauf le nom. Paris: Galilée, 1993. English translation by John P. Leavey, Jr., in *On the Name*, ed. Thomas Dutoit, 89–127. Stanford, Calif.: Stanford University Press, 1995.

Schibboleth pour Paul Celan. Paris: Galilée, 1986. English translation by Joshua Wilner, revised by Thomas Dutoit, as "Schibboleth: For Paul Celan," in *Sovereignties in Question: The Poetics of Paul Celan*, 1–64. New York: Fordham University Press, 2005.

Spectres de Marx. Paris: Galilée, 1993. English translation by Peggy Kamuf, as *Specters of Marx*. New York: Routledge, 1994.

Le toucher: Jean-Luc Nancy. Paris: Galilée, 2000. English translation by Christine Irizarry, as *On Touching—Jean-Luc Nancy*. Stanford, Calif.: Stanford University Press, 2005.

La vérité en peinture. Paris: Flammarion, 1978. English translation by

Geoff Bennington and Ian McLeod, as *The Truth in Painting*. Chicago: University of Chicago Press, 1987.

La voix et le phénomène. Paris: Presses Universitaires de France, 1983 [1967]. English translation by David B. Allison, as *Speech and Phenomena*. Evanston, Ill.: Northwestern University Press, 1973.

Voyous. Paris: Galilée, 2003. English translation by Pascale-Anne Brault and Michael Naas, as *Rogues*. Stanford, Calif.: Stanford University Press, 2005.

Without Alibi. Ed. and trans. Peggy Kamuf. Stanford, Calif.: Stanford University Press. 2002. The French versions of many of these essays can be found in *Jacques Derrida*, ed. Marie-Louise Mallet and Ginette Michaud. Paris: Editions de l'Herne, 2004.

Ulysse Gramophone. Paris: Galilée, 1987.

Articles

"At This Very Moment in This Work Here I Am." In *Re-reading Levinas*, ed. Robert Bernasconi and Simon Critchley, 11-47. Bloomington: Indiana University Press, 1991. Original French in *Psyché: Inventions de l'autre*, 159–202.

"La bête et le souverain." In *La démocratie à venir: Autour de Jacques Derrida*, 433–476. Paris: Galilée, 2004.

"Une certaine possibilité impossible de dire l'événement." In *Dire l'événement, est-ce possible?* 79– 112. Paris: L'Harmattan, 2001.

"Comment ne pas parler: Dénégations (1986). In *Psyché: Inventions de l'autre*, 535–595. Paris: Galilée, 1987. English translation by Ken Frieden, as "How to Avoid Speaking: Denials," in *Languages of the Unsayable*, ed. Sanford Budick and Wolfgang Iser, 3–70. New York: Columbia University Press, 1989.

"Comment nommer." In *Le poète que je cherche à être: Cahier de Michel Deguy*, ed. Yves Charnet, 182–206. Paris: La Table Ronde, 1996.

"Donner la mort." In *L'éthique du don: Jacques Derrida et la pensée du don*, 11–108. Paris: Transition, 1992. English translation by David Wills, as *The Gift of Death*. Chicago: University of Chicago Press, 1995.

"Et cetera . . . (and so on, und so weiter, and so forth, et ainsi de suite, und so überall, etc.)." In *Jacques Derrida*, ed. Marie-Louise

Mallet and Ginette Michaud, 21–34. Paris: Editions de l'Herne, 2004. English translation in *Deconstructions: A User's Guide*, ed. Nicolas Royle, 282–305. London: Palgrave Macmillan, 2000.

"Foi et savoir." In *La Religion*, ed. Jacques Derrida and Gianni Vattimo, 9–86. Paris: Seuil, 1996. English translation by Samuel Weber, as "Faith and Knowledge," in *Religion*, ed. Jacques Derrida and Gianni Vattimo, 1–78. Stanford, Calif.: Stanford University Press, 1998.

"Hospitality." Trans. Gil Anidjar. In Jacques Derrida, *Acts of Religion*, ed. Gil Anidjar, 356–420. London: Routledge, 2002.

"Interprétations à la guerre." In *Psyché II*, 249–305. Paris: Galilée, 2003. English translation by Moshe Ron, as "Interpretations at War," in Jacques Derrida, *Acts of Religion*, ed. Gil Anidjar, 135–188. London: Routledge, 2002.

"Je suis en guerre contre moi-même." Interview in *Le Monde*, August 19, 2004.

"La main de Heidegger (*Geschlecht* II) (1984–1985)." In *Psyché*, 415–452. Paris: Galilée, 1987. English translation by John P. Leavey, Jr., as "*Geschlecht* II: Heidegger's Hand," in *Deconstruction and Philosophy*, ed. John Sallis, 161–196. Chicago: University of Chicago Press, 1987.

"My Chances/Mes Chances: A Rendezvous with Some Epicurean Sterophonies." In *Taking Chances: Derrida, Psychoanalysis, and Literature*, 1–32. Baltimore: Johns Hopkins University Press, 1984.

"Nietzsche and the Machine." Interview with Richard Beardsworth. *Journal of Nietzsche Studies*, no. 7 (Spring 1994): 7–66.

"Nous autres Grecs." In *Nos Grecs et leurs modernes*, 251–276. Paris: Galilée, 1992.

"On Reading Heidegger: An Outline of Remarks to the Essex Colloquium." *Research in Phenomenology* 27 (1987): 171–185.

"L'oreille de Heidegger: Philopolémologie (*Geschlecht* IV)." In *Politiques de l'amitié*, 343–419. Paris: Galilée, 1994. English translation by John P. Leavey, Jr., as "Heidegger's Ear: Philopolemology (Geschlecht IV), in *Reading Heidegger: Commemorations*, ed. John Sallis, 163–218. Bloomington: Indiana University Press, 1993.

"Le ruban de machine à ecrire." In *Papier Machine*, 33–104. Paris: Galilée, 2001. English translation by Peggy Kamuf, as "Typewriter Ribbon," in *Without Alibi*, 71–160.

Derrida Bibliography

www.hydra.umn.edu/derrida/jdind.html

Other Texts

Agamben, Giorgio. *Homo Sacer: Sovereign Power and Bare Life*. Trans. Daniel Heller-Roazen. Stanford, Calif.: Stanford University Press, 1998.

——. *The Open: Man and Animal*. Trans. Kevin Attell. Stanford, Calif.: Stanford University Press, 2004.

——. *Potentialities*. Trans. Daniel Heller-Roazen. Stanford, Calif.: Stanford University Press, 1999.

——. *The Time That Remains*. Trans. Patricia Dailey. Stanford, Calif.: Stanford University Press, 2005.

"L'animal." Special issue, *Alter: Revue de Phénoménologie*, no. 3 (1995).

Beardsworth, Richard. *Derrida and the Political*. New York: Routledge, 1997.

Benjamin, Walter. *Selected Writings*. Vol. 1, *1913–1926*. Ed. Marcus Bullock and Michael W. Jennings. Cambridge: Harvard University Press, 2004.

Bennington, Geoffrey and Jacques Derrida. *Jacques Derrida*. Paris: Seuil, 1991.

Benso, Silvia. *The Face of Things: A Different Side of Ethics*. Albany: SUNY Press, 2000.

Bentham, Jeremy. *The Collected Works of Jeremy Bentham: An Introduction to the Principles of Morals and Legislation*. Ed. J. H. Burns and H. L. A. Hart. Oxford: Clarendon Press, 1996.

Bergson, Henri. *Les deux sources de la morale et de la religion*. In *Œuvres*. Paris: Presses Universitaires de France, 1959. English translation by R. Ashley Audra and Cloudesley Brereton with the assistance of W. Horsfall Carter, as *The Two Sources of Morality and Religion*. Notre Dame: University of Notre Dame Press, 1977 [1935].

Bernasconi, Robert and Simon Critchley, eds. *Re-Reading Levinas*. Bloomington: Indiana University Press, 1991.

Bernasconi, Robert and David Wood, eds. *The Provocation of Levinas*. London: Routledge, 1988.

Blanchot, Maurice. *L'amitié*. Paris: Gallimard, 1971. English translation by Elizabeth Rottenberg, as *Friendship*. Stanford, Calif.: Stanford University Press, 1997.

——. *Death Sentence*. Trans. Lydia Davis. Barrytown, N.Y.: Station Hill, 1978.

——. *L'espace littéraire*. Paris: Gallimard, 1955. English translation by Ann Smock, as *The Space of Literature*. Lincoln: University of Nebraska Press, 1982.

——. *The Step Not Beyond*. Trans. Lycette Nelson. Albany: SUNY Press, 1992.

Bradley, Arthur. *Negative Theology and Modern French Philosophy*. London: Routledge, 2004.

Büchner, Georg. *Büchner: The Complete Plays*. Ed. Michael Patterson. London: Metheun, 2002.

Calarco, Matthew. "On the Borders of Language and Death: Agamben and the Question of the Animal." *Philosophy Today* 44, no. 2 (2000): 91–97.

Calarco, Matthew and Peter Atterton, eds. *Animal Philosophy: Essential Readings in Continental Thought*. London: Continuum International Publishing Group, 2004.

Caputo, John D. *The Prayers and Tears of Jacques Derrida*. Bloomington: Indiana University Press, 1999.

Celan, Paul. *Poems of Paul Celan: Revised and Expanded*. Trans. Michael Hamburger. New York: Persea, 2002.

Cixous, Hélène. *Stigmata: Escaping Texts*. London: Routledge, 1988.

Cixous, Hélène and Jacques Derrida. *Veils*. Trans. Geoff Bennington. Stanford, Calif.: Stanford University Press, 2001.

Crépon, Marc. *Langues sans demeure*. Paris: Galilée, 2005.

Cutrofello, Andrew. *Continental Philosophy: A Contemporary Introduction*. New York: Routledge, 2005.

Dastur, Françoise. *A la naissance des choses*. Fougères la versanne: Encre marine, 2005.

——. *Chair et langage*. Fougères la versanne: Encre marine, 2001.

——. *Comment affronter la mort?* Paris: Bayard, 2005.

——. *Dire le temps*. Fougères la versanne: Encre marine, 1994.

——. "Heidegger et la théologie." *Revue philosophique de Louvain* 92 (1994): 226–245.

——. *La mort*. Paris: Hatier, 1994.

———. *Phénoménologie en questions*. Paris: Vrin, 2004.

DeArmitt, Pleshette and Kas Saghafi, eds. "An Entrusted Responsibility: Reading and Remembering Jacques Derrida." *Epoche: A Special Memorial Issue* 10, no. 2 (Spring 2006).

Deleuze, Gilles. *Différence et répétition*. Paris: Presses Universitaires de France, 1968. English translation by Paul Patton, as *Difference and Repetition*. New York: Columbia University Press, 1994.

———. *Foucault*. Paris: Minuit, 1986. English translation by Paul Bové, as *Foucault*. Minneapolis: University of Minnesota Press, 1988.

———. *Francis Bacon: Logique de la sensation*. Paris: Edition de la différence, 1981. English translation by Daniel W. Smith, as *Francis Bacon: The Logic of Sensation*. Minneapolis: University of Minnesota Press, 2003.

———. *L'île déserte et autres textes*. Paris: Minuit, 2002. English translation by Michael Taormina, as *Desert Islands and Other Texts*. New York: Semiotext(e), 2004.

———. *Logique du sens*. Paris: Minuit, 1969. English translation by Mark Lester with Charles Stivale, as *The Logic of Sense*. New York: Columbia University Press, 1990.

———. *Nietzsche et la philosophie*. Paris: Presses Universitaires de France, 1962. English translation by Hugh Tomlinson, as *Nietzsche and Philosophy*. New York: Columbia University Press, 1983.

———. "Renverser le platonisme." *Revue de métaphysique et de morale* 71, no. 4 (October–December 1966): 426–438.

———. *Spinoza et le problème de l'expression*. Paris: Minuit, 1968. English translation by Martin Joughin, as *Expressionism in Philosophy: Spinoza*. New York: Zone, 1990.

Deleuze, Gilles and Félix Guattari. *Capitalisme et schizophrénie: L'anti-œdipe*. Paris: Minuit, 1972/1973. English translation by Robert Hurley, Mark Seem, and Helen R. Lane, as *Anti-Oedipus: Capitalism and Schizophrenia*. New York: Viking Press, 1977.

———. *Capitalisme et schizophrénie 2: Mille plateaux*. Paris: Minuit, 1980. English translation by Brian Massumi, as *A Thousand Plateaus: Capitalism and Schizophrenia*. Minneapolis: University of Minnesota Press, 1987.

———. *Qu'est-ce que la philosophie?* Paris: Minuit, 1991. English translation by Hugh Tomlinson and Graham Burchell, as *What Is Philosophy?* New York: Columbia University Press, 1994.

Descombes, Vincent. *Modern French Philosophy.* Trans. L. Scott-Fox and J. M. Harding. New York: Cambridge University Press, 1980.

Evans, Fred. *The Multi-Voiced Body: Society, Communication, and the Age of Diversity.* New York: Columbia University Press, forthcoming.

Feldman, Noah. "Islam, Terror and the Second Nuclear Age." *The New York Times Magazine,* October 29, 2006, 50–57, 72, and 76–79.

de Fontenay, Elizabeth. *Le silence des bêtes.* Paris: Fayard, 1998.

——. "Le vivant et l'animal: Entretien avec Elizabeth de Fontenay. Online at www.philagora.net/philo-fac.

Foucault, Michael. *L'archéologie du savoir.* Paris: Gallimard, 1969. English translation by A. M. Sheridan Smith, as *The Archeology of Knowledge.* New York: Pantheon, 1972.

——. "Ceci n'est pas une pipe." In *Dits et écrits,* vol. 1, *1954–1975* (Paris: Gallimard, 2001), pp. 663–678. English translation by James Harnes, as *This Is Not a Pipe.* Berkeley: University of California Press, 1983.

——. *Histoire de la folie.* Paris: Plon, 1961. Partial English translation by Richard Howard, as *Madness and Civilization.* New York: Vintage, 1965.

——. *Histoire de la sexualité I: La volonté de savoir.* Paris: Gallimard, 1976. English translation by Robert Hurley, as *The History of Sexuality: An Introduction, Volume I.* New York: Vintage, 1990.

——. *"Il faut défendre la société": Cours au Collège de France, 1976.* Paris: Gallimard, 1997. English translation by David Macey, as *"Society Must Be Defended": Lectures at the Collège de France, 1975–1976.* New York: Picador, 2003.

——. *Les mots et les choses.* Paris: Gallimard, 1966. English translation anonymous, as *The Order of Things.* New York: Vintage, 1970.

——. *La naissance de la clinique.* Paris: Presses Universitaires de France, 1997 [1963]. English translation by A. M. Sheridan Smith, as *The Birth of the Clinic.* New York: Vintage, 1994.

——. *L'ordre du discours.* Paris: Gallimard, 1971.

——. *Surveiller et punir.* Paris: Gallimard, 1975. English translation by Alan Sheridan, as *Discipline and Punish.* New York: Vintage, 1977.

Gadamer, Hans-Georg. *Gadamer on Celan*. Trans. and ed. by Richard Heinemann and Bruce Krajewski. Albany: SUNY Press, 1997.

Gasché, Rodolphe. *Inventions of Difference: On Jacques Derrida*. Cambridge: Harvard University Press, 1994.

———. *Of Minimal Things: Studies on the Notion of the Relation*. Stanford, Calif.: Stanford University Press, 1999.

———. *The Tain of the Mirror: Derrida and the Philosophy of Reflection*. Cambridge: Harvard University Press, 1986.

Glendinning, Simon. "Heidegger and the Question of Animality." *International Journal of Philosophical Studies* 4, no. 1 (1996): 67–86.

Haddad, Samir. "Inheriting Democracy to Come." In *Theory and Event* 8, no. 1, muse.jhu.edu/demo/theory_and_event/v008/8.1haddad.html.

Hägglund, Martin. "The Necessity of Discrimination: Disjoining Derrida and Levinas." *Diacritics* 34, no. 1 (Spring 2004): 40–71.

Haraway, Donna. *The Companion Species Manifesto: Dogs, People, and Significant Otherness*. Chicago: Prickly Paradigm, 2003.

———. *The Haraway Reader*. London: Routledge, 2004.

Hardt, Michael and Antonio Negri. *Empire*. Cambridge: Harvard University Press, 2000.

Heidegger, Martin. *Basic Problems of Phenomenology*. Trans. Albert Hofstadter. Bloomington: Indiana University Press, 1982.

———. *Basic Writings*. Ed. David Farrell Krell. New York: Harper and Row, 1977.

———. *Early Greek Thinking*. Trans. David Farrell Krell and Frank A. Capuzzi. New York: Harper and Row, 1975.

———. *Ecrits politiques, 1933–1966*. Paris: Gallimard, 1995.

———. *Einfuhrung in die Metaphysik*. Tübingen: Niemeyer, 1987 [1953]. English translation by Ralph Mannheim, as *Introduction to Metaphysics*. New York: Doubleday, 1961.

———. *Gesamtausgabe, Band 29/30, Die Grundbegriffe der Metaphysik, Welt—Endlichkeit—Einsamkeit*. Frankfurt am Main: Klostermann, 1983. English translation by William McNeil and Nicholas Walker, as *The Fundamental Problems of Metaphysics: World, Finitude, Solitude*. Bloomington: Indiana University Press, 1995.

———. *Holzwege*. Frankfurt am Main: Klostermann, 2003.

——. *Identity and Difference.* Trans. Joan Stambaugh. New York: Harper and Row, 1969.

——. *Kant und das Problem der Metaphysik.* Frankfurt am Main: Klostermann, 1973 [1929]. English translation by Richard Taft, as *Kant and the Problem of Metaphysics.* Bloomington: Indiana University Press, 1990.

——. *Nietzsche* 2 vols. Pfullingen: Neske, 1961. English translation by David Farrell Krell, as *Nietzsche.* 4 vols. New York: Harper and Row, 1979–1987.

——. *The Question Concerning Technology and Other Essays.* Trans. J. Glenn Gray. New York: Harper, 1977.

——. *Sein und Zeit.* Tübingen: Niemeyer, 1979 [1927]. English translation by John Macquarrie and Edward Robinson, as *Being and Time.* New York: Harper and Row, 1962. English translation by Joan Stambaugh, as *Being and Time.* Albany: SUNY Press, 1996.

——. "The Self-Assertion of the German University." Trans. Karsten Harries. *Review of Metaphysics* 38, no. 151 (March 1985): 467–502.

——. *Unterwegs zur Sprache.* Pfullingen: Neske, 1982. English translation by Peter D. Hertz, as *On the Way to Language.* New York: Harper and Row, 1971. French translation by Jean Beaufret, Wolfgang Brokmeier, and François Fédier, as *Acheminement vers la parole.* Paris: Gallimard, 1976.

——. *Was Heisst Denken?* Tübingen: Niemeyer, 1961. English translation by J. Glenn Gray, as *What Is Called Thinking?* New York: Harper and Row, 1968. French translation by Gérard Granel, as *Qu'appelle-t-on penser?* Paris: Presses Universitaires de France, 1959.

——. *Wegmarken.* Frankfurt am Main: Klostermann, 1978. English translation by William McNeil, as *Pathmarks.* New York: Cambridge University Press, 1998.

Kant, Immanuel. *Religion Within the Bounds of Reason Alone.* Trans. Theodore M. Greene and Hoyt H. Hudson. New York: Harper and Row, 1960.

Keenan, Dennis. The Question of Sacrifice. Bloomington: Indiana University Press, 2005.

Kornbluth, Hilary, ed. *Naturalizing Epistemology.* Cambridge, Mass.: MIT Press, 1987.

Krell, David Farrell. *Daimon Life: Heidegger and Life-Philosophy*. Bloomington: Indiana University Press, 1992.

Lacan, Jacques. *Ecrits*. Paris: Seuil, 1966. Partial English translation by Alan Sheridan, as *Ecrits: A Selection*. New York: Norton, 1977.

———. *Les quatres concepts fondamentaux de la psychanalyse*. Paris: Seuil, Essais, 1973. English translation by Alan Sheridan, as *The Four Fundamental Concepts of Psycho-Analysis*. New York: Norton, 1978.

Lampert, Jay. *Deleuze and Guattari's Philosophy of History*. London: Continuum, 2006.

Lawlor, Leonard. *The Challenge of Bergsonism: Phenomenology, Ontology, Ethics*. London: Continuim, 2003.

———. "Derrida." In *The Stanford University Encyclopedia of Philosophy*, 2006, plato.stanford.edu.

———. *Derrida and Husserl: The Basic Problem of Phenomenology*. Bloomington: Indiana University Press, 2002.

———. *Imagination and Chance: The Difference Between the Thought of Ricœur and Derrida*. Albany: SUNY Press, 1992.

———. *The Implications of Immanence: Toward a New Concept of Life*. New York: Fordham University Press, 2006.

———. *Thinking Through French Philosophy: The Being of the Question*. Bloomington: Indiana University Press, 2003.

Levinas, Emmanuel. *Autrement qu'être ou au-delà de l'essence*. The Hague: Martinus Nijhoff, 1974. English translation by Alphonso Lingis, as *Otherwise than Being or Beyond Essence*. The Hague: Martinus Nijhoff, 1981.

———. *Collected Philosophical Papers*. Trans. Alphonso Lingis. The Hague: Martinus Nijhoff, 1987.

———. *Humanisme de l'autre homme*. Paris: Fata Morgana, 1972. English translation by Nidra Poller, as *Humanism of the Other*. Urbana-Champagne: University of Illinois Press, 2003.

———. *Totalité et infini*. The Hague: Martinus Nijhoff, 1961. English translation by Alphonso Lingis, as *Totality and Infinity*. Pittsburgh: Duquesne University Press, 1969.

Lévi-Strauss, Claude. *Totemism*. Trans. Rodney Needham. Boston: Beacon, 1963.

Llewelyn, John. "Am I Obsessed by Bobby?" In *Re-Reading Levinas*, ed. Robert Bernasconi and Simon Critchley, 234–245. Bloomington: Indiana University Press, 1991.

——. *The Middle Voice of Ecological Conscience*. New York: St. Martin's, 1991.

Macey, David. *The Lives of Michel Foucault*. New York: Vintage, 1995.

Malabou, Catherine. *Que faire de notre cerveau?* Paris: Bayard, 2004.

Mallet, Marie-Louise, d. *L'animal autobiographique: Autour de Jacques Derrida*. Paris: Galilée, 1999.

——. *Le passage des frontières*. Paris: Galilée, 1994.

Marion, Jean-Luc. *Réduction et donation*. Paris: Presses Universitaires de France, 1989.

Marrati-Guénoun, Paola. *La genèse et la trace: Derrida lecteur de Husserl et Heidegger*. Dordrecht: Kluwer, 1998.

Massignon, Louis. *L'hospitalité sacrée*. Paris: Nouvelle Cité, 1987.

Merleau-Ponty, Maurice. *Humanisme et terreur*. Paris: Idées/Gallimard, 1980 [1947]. English translation by John O'Neill, as *Humanism and Terror*. Boston: Beacon, 1969.

——. *La nature: Notes cours du Collège de France*. Ed. Dominque Séglard. Paris: Seuil, 1995. English translation by Robert Vallier, as *Nature: Course Notes from the Collège de France*. Evanston, Ill.: Northwestern University Press, 2003.

——. *Le visible et l'invisible*. Paris: Gallimard, 1964. English translation by Alphonso Lingis, as *The Visible and the Invisible*. Evanston, Ill.: Northwestern University Press, 1968.

Michelfelder, Diane P. and Richard E. Palmer. *Dialogue and Deconstruction: The Gadamer-Derrida Encounter*. Albany: SUNY Press, 1989.

Naas, Michael. *Taking on the Tradition: Jacques Derrida and the Legacies of Deconstruction*. Stanford, Calif.. Stanford University Press, 2003

Nagel, Thomas. *Mortal Questions*. New York: Cambridge University Press, 2006.

Nancy, Jean-Luc. *La déclosion*. Vol. 1, *Déconstruction du christianisme*. Paris: Galilée, 2005.

——. "La deconstruction du christianisme." *Les Etudes Philosophiques*, no. 4 (1998): 503–519. English translation by Simon Sparks, as "The Deconstruction of Christianity," in *Religion and Media*, ed. Hent

De Vries and Samuel Weber, 112–130. Stanford, Calif.: Stanford University Press, 2001.

Oliver, Kelly. *The Colonization of Psychic Space: A Psychoanalytic Social Theory of Oppression*. Minneapolis: University of Minnesota Press, 2004.

Patton, Paul. *Deleuze and the Political*. London: Routledge, 2000.

Patton, Paul and John Protevi, eds. *Deleuze and Derrida*. London: Continuum, 2003.

Raffoul, François. "Derrida et l'éthique de l'im-possible." Forthcoming in a special issue of *Revue de métaphysique et de morale* on Derrida.

Regan, Tom. *The Case for Animal Rights*. Berkeley: University of California Press, 1985.

——, ed. *Animal Sacrifice: Religious Perspectives on the Use of Animals in Science*. Philadelphia: Temple University Press, 1986.

Rosset, Clément. *Logique du pire: Elément pour une philosophie tragique*. Paris: Presses Universitaires de France, 1971.

Royle, Nicolas, ed. *Deconstructions: A User's Guide*. London: Palgrave Macmillan, 2000.

Russon, John and John Sallis, eds. *Retracing the Platonic Text*. Evanston, Ill.: Northwestern University Press, 2000.

Sallis, John. *Chorology: On Beginning in Plato's Timaeus*. Bloomington: Indiana University Press, 1999.

——, ed. *Deconstruction and Philosophy*. Chicago: University of Chicago Press, 1987.

Schmitt, Carl. *The Concept of the Political*. Trans. George Schwab. Chicago: University of Chicago Press, 1996.

——. *The Crisis of Parliamentary Democracy*. Trans. Ellen Kennedy. Cambridge, Mass.: MIT Press, 2000.

——. *Political Theology*. Trans. George Schwab. Cambridge, Mass.: MIT Press, 1988.

Schmidt, Dennis. *On Germans and Other Greeks*. Bloomington: Indiana University Press, 2002.

Schrift, Alan. *Twentieth Century French Philosophy: Key Themes and Thinkers*. Oxford: Blackwell, 2006.

Singer, Peter. *Animal Liberation*. New York: HarperCollins, 2002 [1975].

——. *The Expanding Circle: Ethics and Sociobiology*. New York: Farrar, Strauss and Giroux, 1981.

———. *One World.* 2d ed. New Haven: Yale University Press, 2004.

———, ed. *In Defense of Animals: The Second Wave.* Oxford: Blackwell, 2006.

Steeves, H. Peter, ed. *Animal Others: On Ethics, Ontology, and Animal Life.* Albany: SUNY Press, 1999.

Toadvine, Ted. "How Not to Be a Jellyfish: Human Exceptionalism and the Ontology of Reflection." In "Phenomenology and the Non-Human Animal," ed. Christian Lotz and Corinne Painter. Under review with Springer Academic Publishers.

———. "'Strange Kinship': Merleau-Ponty on the Human-Animal Relation." *Phenomenology of Life—From the Animal Soul to the Human Mind.* Vol. 1, *In Search of Experience,* pp. 17–32. Analecta Husserliana 93. Dordrecht: Springer, 2006.

Wolfe, Cary. *Animal Rites: American Culture, the Discourse of Species, and Posthumanist Theory.* Chicago: University of Chicago Press, 2003.

———, ed. *Zoontologies: The Question of the Animal.* Minneapolis: University of Minnesota Press, 2003.

Wood, David. "Comment ne pas manger." In *Animal Others: On Ethics, Ontology, and Animal Life,* ed. H. Peter Steeves, 15–35. Albany: SUNY Press, 1999.

———. *The Step Back: Ethics and Politics after Deconstruction.* Albany: SUNY Press, 2005.

———, ed. *Derrida: A Critical Reader.* Cambridge, Mass.: Blackwell, 1994.

———. *Of Derrida, Heidegger, and Spirit.* Evanston, Ill.: Northwestern University Press, 1993.

Wood, David and Robert Bernasconi, eds. *Derrida and Différance.* Evanston, Ill.: Northwestern University Press, 1988.

INDEX